MW00339520

ARCHI-GRAPHIC

Published in 2015 by
Laurence King Publishing Ltd
361–373 City Road
London EC1V 1LR

e-mail: enquiries@laurenceking.com
www.laurenceking.com

© Text and illustrations 2015 Frank Jacobus

This book was designed and produced by
Laurence King Publishing Ltd, London.

Frank Jacobus has asserted his right under
the Copyright, Designs and Patents Act of 1988
to be identified as the author of this work.

All rights reserved. No part of this publication
may be reproduced or transmitted in any form or
by any means, electronic or mechanical, including
photocopy, recording or any information storage
and retrieval system, without prior permission
in writing from the publisher.

A catalogue record for this book is available
from the British Library.

ISBN: 978-1-78067-619-7

Book Design: Alexandre Coco
Senior Editor: Peter Jones

Printed in China

ARCHI-GRAPHIC

AN INFOGRAPHIC LOOK AT ARCHITECTURE

Frank Jacobus

Laurence King Publishing

contents

ARCHI-GRAPHIC
An Infographic Operation on Architecture

What type of architecture do dictators prefer? What would a subway map of the affairs of famous architects look like? What is the current state of gender and ethnic diversity within the profession? Which architects would win a color war, Dutch or American? *Archi-Graphic* places architecture on the operating table, using infographics to cut a visual cross-section that answers these questions and many more. I began this project in the spring of 2013 because I was desperate to read this kind of book, and I had found no other resource quite like it. The intention behind *Archi-Graphic* is that knowledge of the richness and complexity inherent in the discipline and profession of architecture can become an accessible and even desirable pursuit for architects and non-architects alike. This book aims to be educational without being especially didactic, and though it embraces certain serious themes, it is not so severe that it can't poke fun at itself once in a while. *Archi-Graphic* peers into issues within architecture that are rarely if ever tackled in an accessible way: big personalities, color relationships in the built environment, gender and ethnicity in the profession, construction expense, even death, are visually revealed through colorful infographic diagrams. My hope is that people will be drawn to this book first because of its graphic quality, but will ultimately enjoy it because of its compelling content and inherent complexities. What other architecture book provides a map of every project that Le Corbusier ever built and in the location and order that he built them, presented to us as the flight of a bird? If you enjoy architecture, graphic design, art, information graphics, or simply love visual complexity, this book should suit you well.

architectural migration...

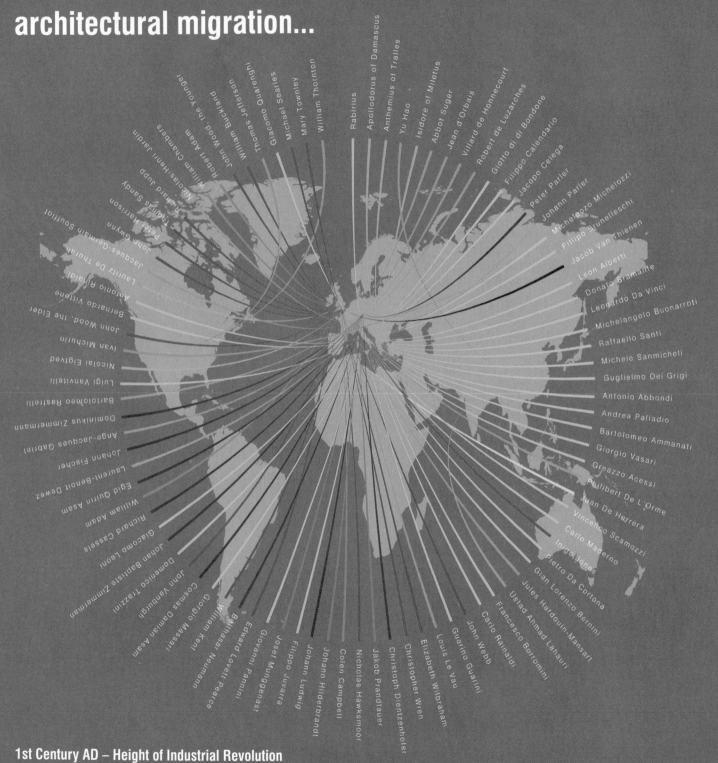

1st Century AD – Height of Industrial Revolution

Giuseppe Piermarini
James Bloodworth
Joseph Lillie
James Hoban
Benjamin Latrobe
Charles Percier
Joseph Ramee
Ithiel Town
John Soane
John Nash
Charles Bulfinch
Asher Benjamin
Carlo Rossi
Samuel McIntire
Barthelemy Lafon
Vasily Stasov
William Wilkins
Alexander Parris
Karl Schinkel
Giuseppe Jappelli
Leo Von Klenze
John Dobson
Robert Mills
Ignatius Bonomi
Auguste De Montferrand
William Burn
Lewis Cubbitt
William Strickland
Philip Charles Hardwick
Constantine Ton
Sir Charles Barry
Thomas Donaldson
Enrico Marconi
Richard Lane
George Webster
Ammi Young
William Hosking
Joseph Paxton
Henri Labrouste
Decimus Burton
Kolyu Ficheto
Richard Upjohn
Sir James Pennethorne
Gottfried Semper
Henry Austin
David Bryce
Alexander Jackson Davis
Thomas U. Walter
Thomas Henry Wyatt
Carlo Bassi
A. W. N. Pugin
Samuel Sanders Teulon
Eugene Viollet-le-Duc
Gridley James Fox Bryant
Edward Clark
George Devey
James Renwick, Jr.
Frederick Marrable
Sir Horace Jones
Frederick Law Olmsted
Edward Middleton Barry
Adolf Cluss
Thomas Fuller
Jacob Snyder
William Burges
Pierre Cuypers
Henry Engelbert
Charles Garnier
Richard Hunt
George Hunt
Thomas Edmund Street
George Edmund Street
Olart Tissen
Thomas Alexander Tefft
John Wornham Penfold
James Fowler
Calvert Vaux
Thomas Worthington
Charles Barry, Jr.
J. L. Stevenson
Alfred Waterhouse
William Morris
Alfred B. Mullett
Edward William Grayson
George Enoch Grayson
Frederic Auguste Bartholdi
Camillo Boito
Samuel Hannaford
J. Cleavland Cady
Henry Hobson Richardson
Frank Furness
Archimedes Russell
Otto Wagner
Watson Fothergill
Edward Alexander Wyon
Basil Champneys
Dankmar Adler
John A. B. Koch
Charles Follen McKim
Benno Janssen
Joseph Lyman Silsbee
R. Newton Breeze
John Root
Silvanus Trevail
Stanford White
Charles Bickel
Will Price
Thomas Hastings
Victoria Horta
Albert Pretzinger
Frederick J. Osterling
Oskar Marmorek
Charles F. Lembke
Frank Lloyd Wright
Louis Kamper Oldrich
Joseph Maria Olbrich
Joseph Bick
William Alexander Harvey
William Groggins
S. N. Cooke
Walter Gropius
Ludwig Mies van der Rohe

Bauhaus – Arcosanti

Arcosanti – Present

11

20th-century master palettes

What happens when you eliminate building form and focus purely on the color in an architect's material palette? The diagrams on this spread and the following extract material colors from the chosen architect's major works to form a color wheel of their careers. Follow the page numbers in the center of the color wheels for a more detailed look at the projects, the time in the architect's career they were produced, and relative quantities of materials used in the built works.

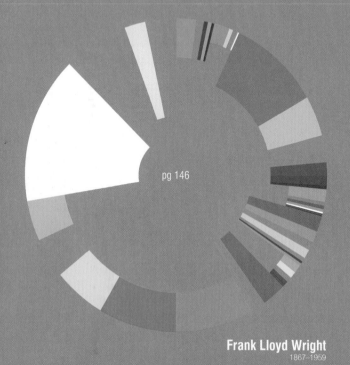

pg 146

Frank Lloyd Wright
1867–1959

pg 147

Erik Gunnar Asplund
1885–1940

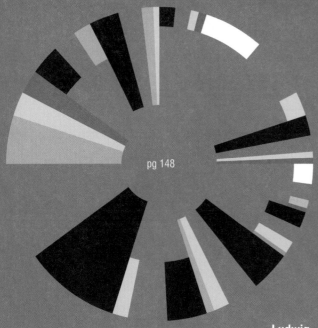

pg 148

**Ludwig
Mies van der Rohe**
1886–1969

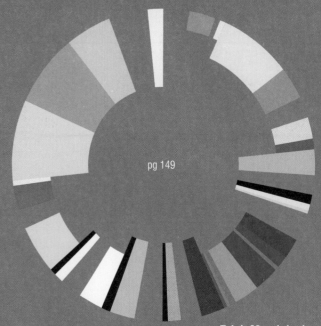

pg 149

Erich Mendelsohn
1887–1953

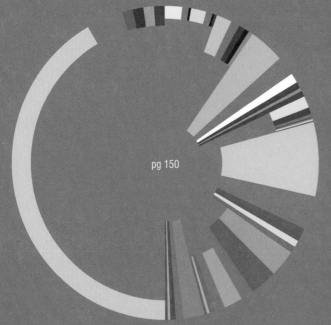

pg 150

Le Corbusier
1887–1965

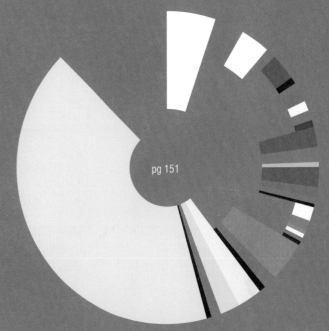

pg 151

Alvar Aalto
1898–1976

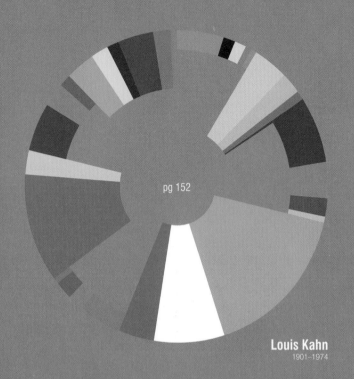

pg 152

Louis Kahn
1901–1974

pg 153

Luis Barragán
1902–1988

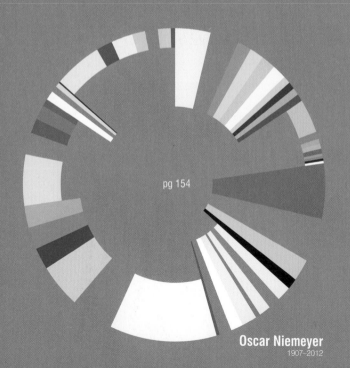

pg 154

Oscar Niemeyer
1907–2012

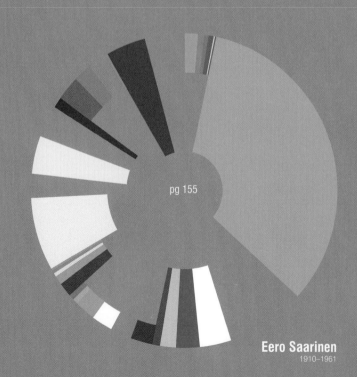

pg 155

Eero Saarinen
1910–1961

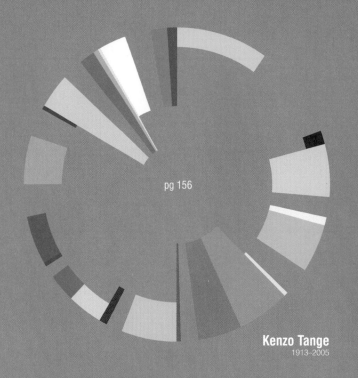

pg 156

Kenzo Tange
1913–2005

pg 157

Lina Bo Bardi
1914–1992

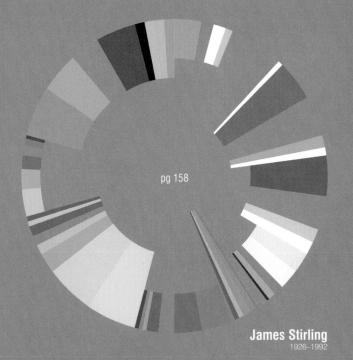

pg 158

James Stirling
1926–1992

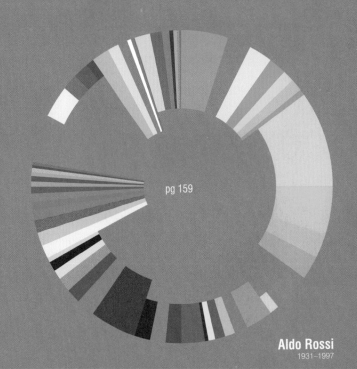

pg 159

Aldo Rossi
1931–1997

what type of architecture do dictators prefer?

Mapping architectural preferences through multiple personalities, the colored dots represent architectural styles present in the dictator's country prior to and during their rule, while the colored rings represent the time period of their reign and the type of dictatorial rule.

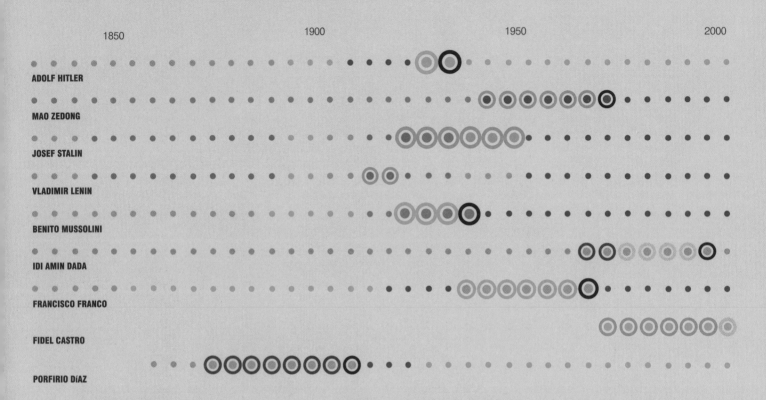

1850   1900   1950   2000

ADOLF HITLER

MAO ZEDONG

JOSEF STALIN

VLADIMIR LENIN

BENITO MUSSOLINI

IDI AMIN DADA

FRANCISCO FRANCO

FIDEL CASTRO

PORFIRIO DíAZ

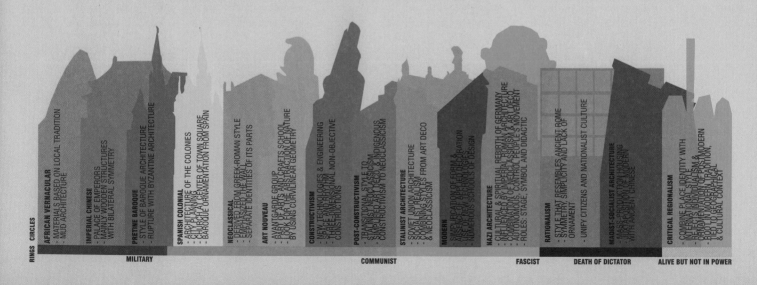

RINGS   CIRCLES

AFRICAN VERNACULAR
- MATERIALS BASED ON LOCAL TRADITION
- MUD ARCHITECTURE

IMPERIAL CHINESE
- PALACE OF EMPERORS
- MAINLY WOODEN STRUCTURES WITH BILATERAL SYMMETRY

PRETINE BAROQUE
- STYLE OF BAROQUE ARCHITECTURE
- RUPTURE WITH BYZANTINE ARCHITECTURE

SPANISH COLONIAL
- ARCHITECTURE OF THE COLONIES
- CITY PLANNING
- ARCHITECTURAL CENTER OF TOWN SQUARE
- BAROQUE ORNAMENTATION FROM SPAIN

NEOCLASSICAL
- DERIVED FROM GREEK-ROMAN STYLE
- EMPHASIZED THE WALL
- SEPARATE IDENTITIES OF ITS PARTS

ART NOUVEAU
- AVANTGARDE GROUP
- ARTS AND CRAFTS SCHOOL
- LOOK FOR THE ABSTRACTION OF NATURE BY USING CURVILINEAR GEOMETRY

CONSTRUCTIVISM
- NEW TECHNOLOGIES & ENGINEERING
- SPACE AND RHYTHM
- THREE-DIMENSIONAL NON-OBJECTIVE CONSTRUCTIONS

POST-CONSTRUCTIVISM
- TRANSITIONAL STYLE TO STALINIST NEOCLASSICISM
- SIMPLIFIED ART DECO TO NEOCLASSICISM
- CONSTRUCTIVISM TO NEOCLASSICISM

STALINIST ARCHITECTURE
- SOVIET UNION ARCHITECTURE
- SOCIALIST REALISM
- COMBINING STYLES FROM ART DECO & NEOCLASSICISM

MODERN
- SIMPLIFICATION OF FORM &
- ABSENCE OF APPLIED DECORATION
- USE OF NEW TECHNOLOGIES
- NUMEROUS SCHOOLS OF DESIGN

NAZI ARCHITECTURE
- CULTURAL & SPIRITUAL REBIRTH OF GERMANY
- INFLUENCE BY IMPERIAL ROMAN ARCHITECTURE
- COMBINATION OF NEOCLASSICISM & ART DECO
- AUTONOMOUS, CONTROL PEOPLE'S MOVEMENT
- ROLES: STAGE, SYMBOL AND DIDACTIC

RATIONALISM
- STYLE THAT RESEMBLES ANCIENT ROME
- SYMMETRY, SIMPLICITY AND LACK OF ORNAMENT
- UNIFY CITIZENS AND NATIONALIST CULTURE

MAOIST-SOCIALIST ARCHITECTURE
- MASS-PRODUCTION HOUSING
- COMBINATION OF MODERN WITH ANCIENT CHINESE

CRITICAL REGIONALISM
- COMBINE PLACE IDENTITY WITH INTERNATIONALISM
- REJECT BOTH NOSTALGIC HISTORICISM & PLAIN DECORATIVE
- PROPOSE MODERN TRADITION, ROOTED TO GEOGRAPHICAL & CULTURAL CONTEXT

MILITARY   COMMUNIST   FASCIST   DEATH OF DICTATOR   ALIVE BUT NOT IN POWER

Adolf Hitler
26.7%
[17,000,000]

Benito Mussolini
1.1%
[700,000]

Francisco Franco
0.3%
[200,000]

Porfirio Díaz
0.01%
[6,800]

Mao Zedong
100%
[+70,000,000]

Vladimir Lenin
1.6%
[1,000,000]

Fidel Castro
0.1%
[73,000]

Idi Amin Dada
0.8%
[500,000]

Josef Stalin
36.2%
[23,000,000]

the blood percentage

Amount of people killed in relation to Mao Zedong's death toll

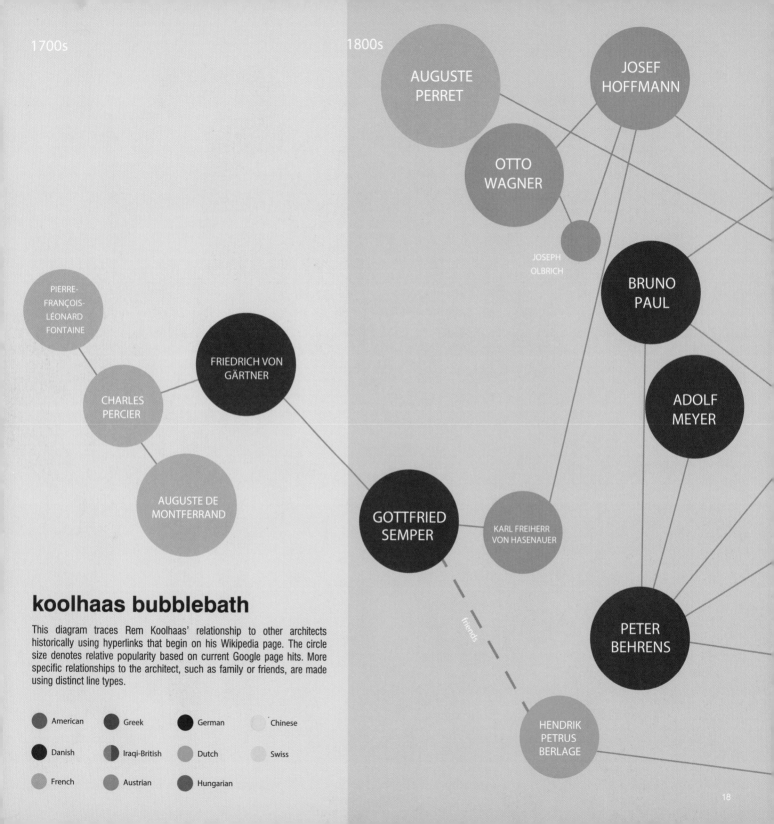

1700s

1800s

AUGUSTE PERRET

JOSEF HOFFMANN

OTTO WAGNER

JOSEPH OLBRICH

BRUNO PAUL

PIERRE-FRANÇOIS-LÉONARD FONTAINE

FRIEDRICH VON GÄRTNER

ADOLF MEYER

CHARLES PERCIER

AUGUSTE DE MONTFERRAND

GOTTFRIED SEMPER

KARL FREIHERR VON HASENAUER

friends

PETER BEHRENS

koolhaas bubblebath

This diagram traces Rem Koolhaas' relationship to other architects historically using hyperlinks that begin on his Wikipedia page. The circle size denotes relative popularity based on current Google page hits. More specific relationships to the architect, such as family or friends, are made using distinct line types.

HENDRIK PETRUS BERLAGE

- American
- Greek
- German
- Chinese
- Danish
- Iraqi-British
- Dutch
- Swiss
- French
- Austrian
- Hungarian

KEM
WEBER

MICHAEL
GRAVES

JOHN
HEJDUK

MARCEL
BREUER

RICHARD
MEIER

LE CORBUSIER

PETER
EISENMAN

friends

ZAHA
HADID

CHARLES
GWATHMEY

MIES
VAN DER
ROHE

I. M. PEI

ELIA
ZENGHELIS

REM
KOOLHAAS

friends

BJARKE
INGELS

WALTER
GROPIUS

family

DIRK
ROOSENBURG

JOSHUA PRINCE-
RAMUS

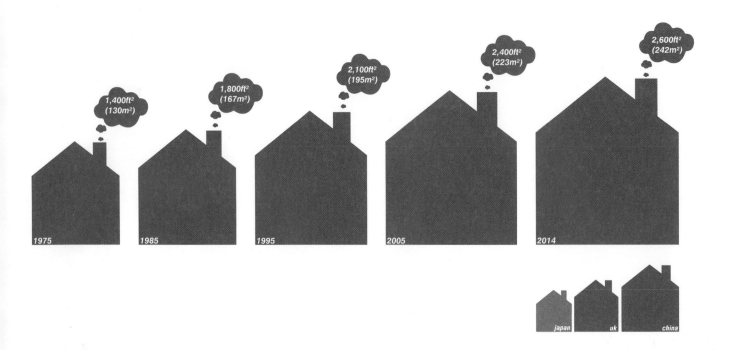

a man's home is his castle

...and castles in the United States have been growing.
This diagram tracks the growth of home sizes in the United States in recent history
and compares the current home size in the US to that of Japan, the UK, and China.

the architecture of affairs

A subway map of the extramarital affairs of famous architects.

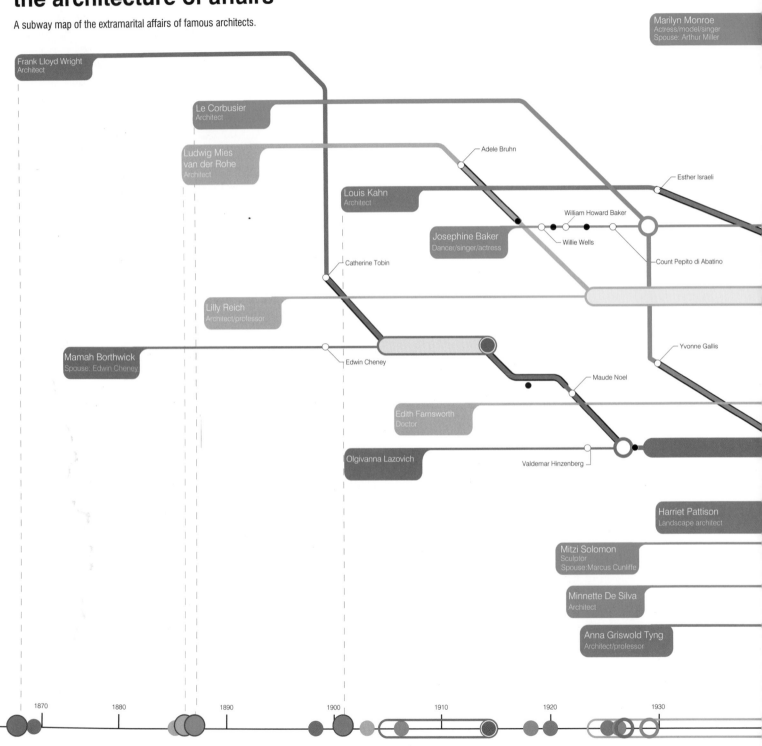

Marilyn Monroe
Actress/model/singer
Spouse: Arthur Miller

Frank Lloyd Wright
Architect

Le Corbusier
Architect

Ludwig Mies
van der Rohe
Architect

Louis Kahn
Architect

Adele Bruhn

Esther Israeli

William Howard Baker

Josephine Baker
Dancer/singer/actress

Willie Wells

Count Pepito di Abatino

Catherine Tobin

Lilly Reich
Architect/professor

Mamah Borthwick
Spouse: Edwin Cheney

Edwin Cheney

Yvonne Gallis

Maude Noel

Edith Farnsworth
Doctor

Olgivanna Lazovich

Valdemar Hinzenberg

Harriet Pattison
Landscape architect

Mitzi Solomon
Sculptor
Spouse:Marcus Cunliffe

Minnette De Silva
Architect

Anna Griswold Tyng
Architect/professor

1870   1880   1890   1900   1910   1920   1930

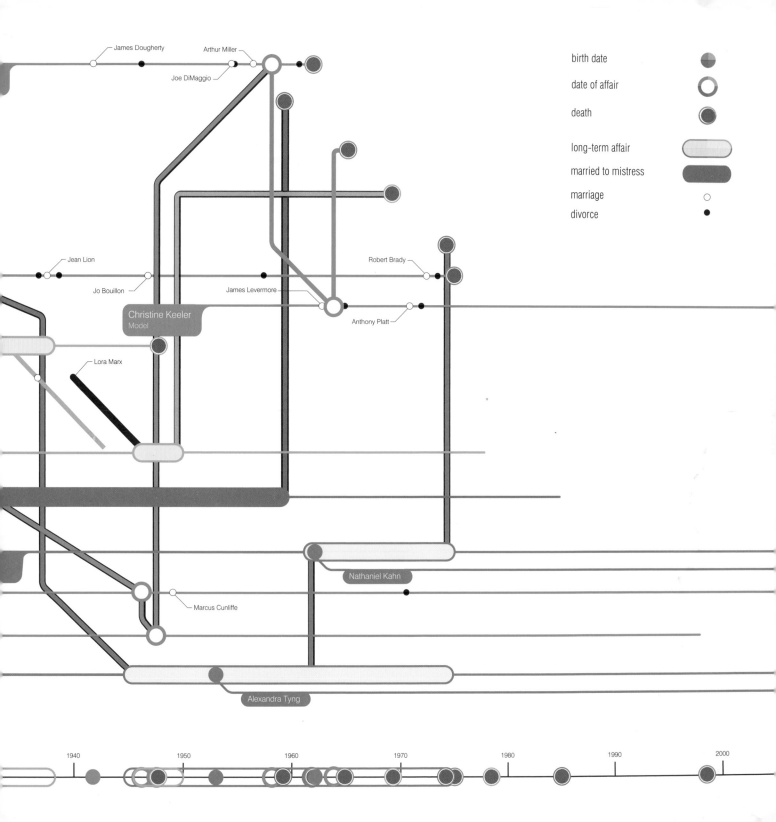

birth date

date of affair

death

long-term affair

married to mistress

marriage

divorce

James Dougherty

Arthur Miller

Joe DiMaggio

Jean Lion

Jo Bouillon

Robert Brady

James Levermore

Christine Keeler
Model

Anthony Platt

Lora Marx

Nathaniel Kahn

Marcus Cunliffe

Alexandra Tyng

1940   1950   1960   1970   1980   1990   2000

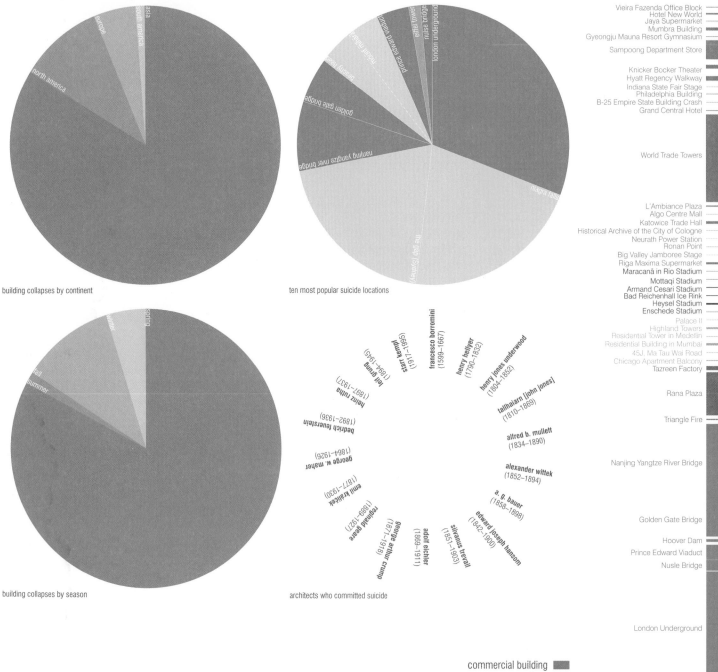

building collapses by continent

ten most popular suicide locations

building collapses by season

architects who committed suicide

death by architecture

Mapping death by suicide and building collapse.

commercial building
stadium
residential
factory

bridge
building
monument/landmark

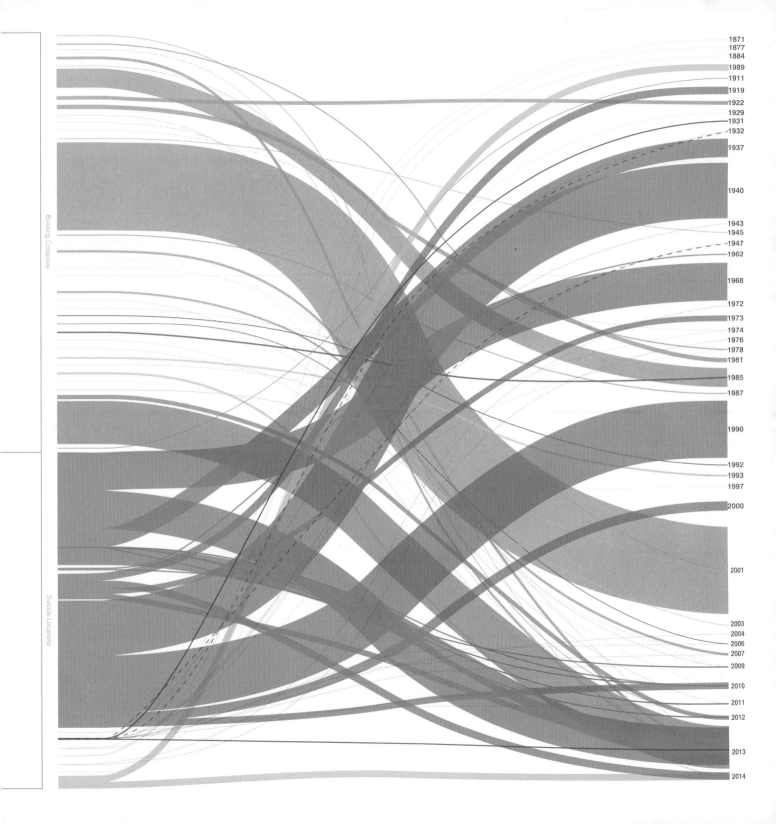

Goetz Collection, 1992
Swiss Federal Railway Switchtower, 1997
Institute for Hospital Pharmaceuticals, 1998
Küppersmühle Museum, 1999
Dominus Winery, 1999
Rue des Suisses, 2000

Tate Modern, 2000

St Jakob Park, 2001

REHAB, 2002

Laban Dance Centre, 2003
Laurenz Foundation Schaulager, 2003

Forum Building, 2004

IKMZ Cottbus, 2004

M. H. de Young Memorial Museum, 2005

Walker Art Center, 2005

Allianz Arena, 2005

40 Bond Street, London, 2007

Beijing National Stadium, 2008

CaixaForum Madrid, 2008
Tenerife Espacio de las Artes, 2008
VitraHaus, 2009
Museum der Kulturen, Basel, 2010

Parrish Art Museum, 2012

Pérez Art Museum Miami, 2013

Ricola Storage Building, 1987
Library of the Eberswalde Technical School, 1996

Prada Aoyama Epicenter, 2003

Herzog & de Meuron chromachrono

Jacques Herzog & Pierre de Meuron (1978–present)
Selected works, 1987–2013.

House I, 1968
House III, 1971

House II, 1970
House VI, 1975

IBA Social Housing, 1985

Firehouse for Engine Co.233 & Ladder Co.176, 1985

Wexner Center for the Visual Arts, 1989

Groningen Music-Video Pavilion, 1990

Aronoff Center for Design & Art, 1996

Koizumi Sangyo Office Building, 1990

Nunotani Office Building, 1992

Greater Columbus Convention Center, 1993

Aachen Bus Shelter, 1996

Memorial to the Murdered Jews of Europe, 2005

University of Phoenix Stadium, 2006

Library of Galicia & Galician Archive, 2011

Eisenman Architects chromachrono

Peter Eisenman (1960–present)
Selected works, 1968–2001.

Shigeru Ban Architects chromachrono

Shigeru Ban (1985–present)
Selected works, 1991–2013.

Library of a Poet, 1991
Housing at Shakujii Park, 1992
Complex by the Railroad, 1992
Factory at Hamura-Dengyosha, 1993
Miyake Design Studio Gallery, 1994
Curtain Wall House, 1995
Nine Square Grid House, 1997
Tazawako Station, 1997
Ivy Structure, 1999
Naked House, 2000
GC Osaka Building, 2000
Imai Hospital Daycare Center, 2001
Bamboo Furniture House, 2002
Atsushi Imai Memorial Gymnasium, 2002
Paper Art Museum, 2002
Nomadic Museum in New York, 2005
Maison E, 2006
Sagaponac House, 2006
Papertainer Museum, 2006
Artek Pavilion, 2007
Nicolas G. Hayek Center, 2007
Crescent House, 2008
Villa Vista, 2010
Centre Pompidou-Metz, 2010
Container Temporary Housing, 2011
Metal Shutter House, 2011
Paper Concert Hall, 2011
Villa at Sengokubara, 2013
Tameda Office Building, 2013
Cardboard Cathedral Christchurch, 2013

House for Vocalists, 1991
Furniture House 1, 1995
Paper Log House, 1995
Picture Window House, 2002
Glass Shutter House, 2003
Furniture House 6 (Make It Right), 2009
Yakushima Takatsuka Lodge, 2013

african american 1%

asian/pacific islander 5%

other 1%

aian't ethnic

A representation of the current ethnic distribution of registered architect members within the American Institute of Architects.

unknown 18%

hispanic 3%

caucasian 72%

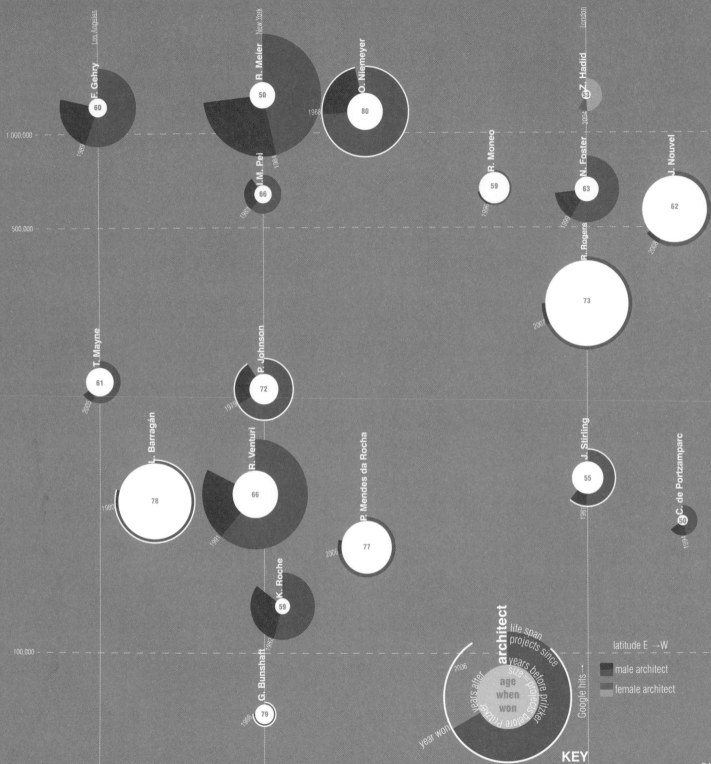

F. Gehry — Los Angeles
60
1989

R. Meier — New York
50
1988

O. Niemeyer
80

I.M. Pei
66
1984
1983

Z. Hadid — London
53
2004

R. Moneo
59
1996

N. Foster
63
1999

J. Nouvel
62
2008

R. Rogers
73
2007

T. Mayne
61
2005

P. Johnson
72
1979

L. Barragán
78
1980

R. Venturi
66
1991

P. Mendes da Rocha
77
2006

J. Stirling
55
1981

C. de Portzamparc
50
1994

K. Roche
59
1982

G. Bunshaft
79
1988

1,000,000
500,000
100,000

KEY

architect

life span
projects since
years before pritzker
size · projects before Pritzker
age when won
years after
year won
2006
Google hits

latitude E → W

■ male architect
■ female architect

34

anatomizing the Pritzker

This diagram tracks the winners of the Pritzker Prize, one of architecture's most prestigious awards.

aphorisms on the operating table

In the spirit of the architect's love of the diagram, the famous architectural aphorisms on this spread and the next one have been placed on the operating table, each becoming its own space and form through this act of sentence dissection.

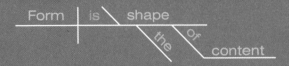

"Form is the shape of content."
Ben Shahn

"Less is more."
Ludwig Mies van der Rohe

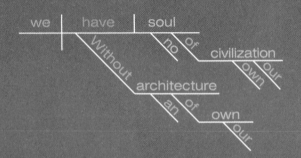

"Without an architecture of our own we have no soul of our own civilization."
Frank Lloyd Wright

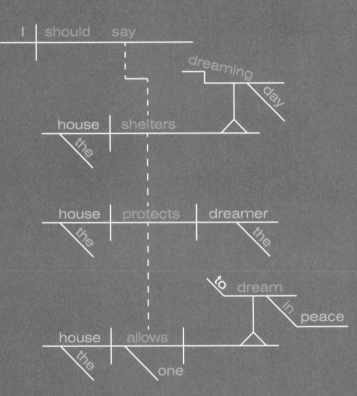

"I should say: the house shelters day dreaming, the house protects the dreamer, the house allows one to dream in peace."
Gaston Bachelard

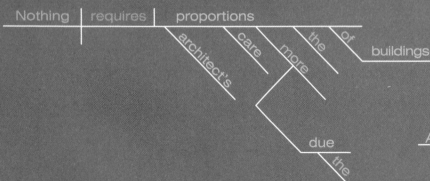

"Nothing requires the architect's care more than the due proportions of buildings."
Vitruvius

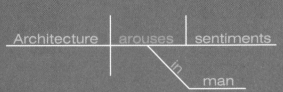

"Architecture arouses sentiments in man."
Adolf Loos

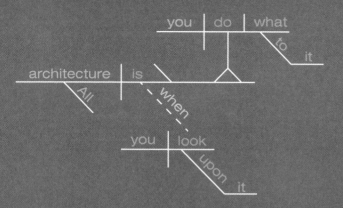

"All architecture is what you do to it when you look upon it."
Walt Whitman

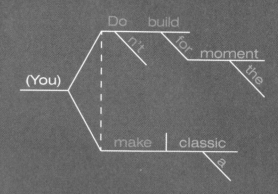

"Don't build for the moment...make a classic."
Michael Graves

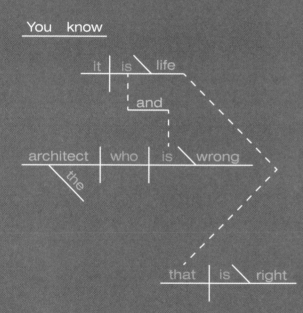

"You know, it is life that is right and the architect who is wrong."
Le Corbusier

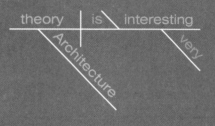

"Architecture theory is very interesting."
David Byrne

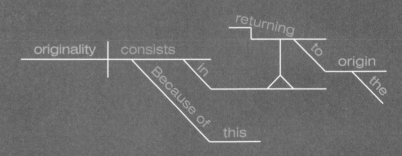

"Because of this, originality consists in returning to the origin."
Antoni Gaudi

"Form follows function."
Louis Sullivan

noun   verb   pronoun   adjective   preposition   adverb   conjunction

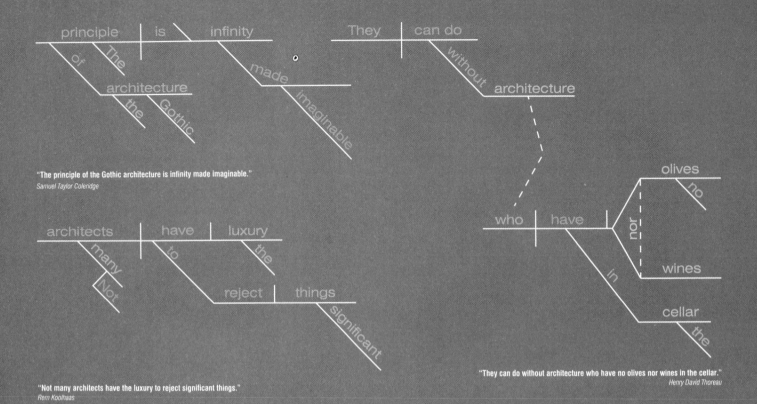

"The principle of the Gothic architecture is infinity made imaginable."
Samuel Taylor Coleridge

"They can do without architecture who have no olives nor wines in the cellar."
Henry David Thoreau

"Not many architects have the luxury to reject significant things."
Rem Koolhaas

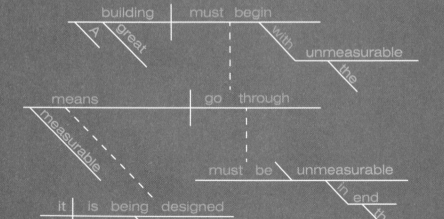

"A great building must begin with the unmeasurable, go through measurable means
when it is being designed, and in the end must be unmeasurable."
Louis Kahn

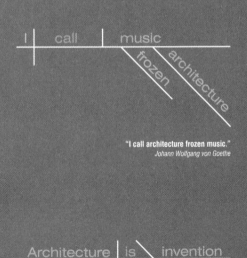

"I call architecture frozen music."
Johann Wolfgang von Goethe

"Architecture is invention."
Oscar Niemeyer

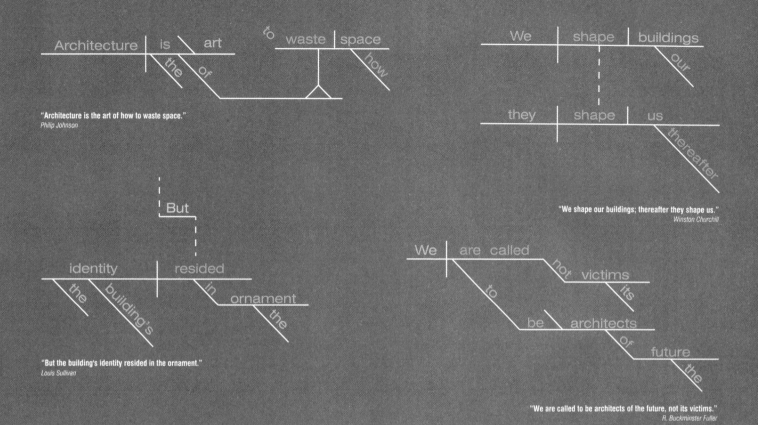

"Architecture is the art of how to waste space."
Philip Johnson

"We shape our buildings; thereafter they shape us."
Winston Churchill

"But the building's identity resided in the ornament."
Louis Sullivan

"We are called to be architects of the future, not its victims."
R. Buckminster Fuller

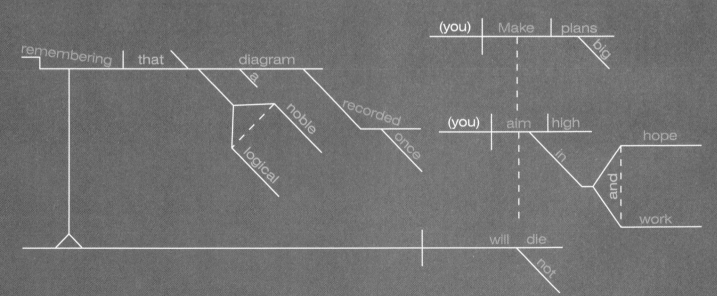

"Make big plans; aim high in hope and work, remembering that a noble, logical diagram once recorded will not die."
Daniel Burnham

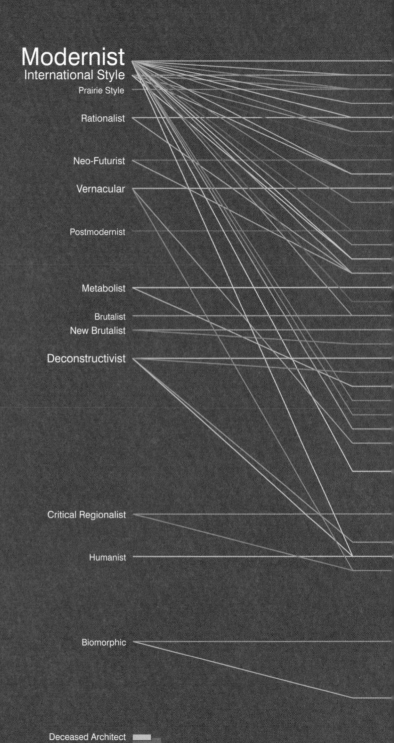

Modernist
International Style

Prairie Style

Rationalist

Neo-Futurist

Vernacular

Postmodernist

Metabolist

Brutalist
New Brutalist

Deconstructivist

Critical Regionalist

Humanist

Biomorphic

architects quantified

Age, number of projects, internet popularity, and tallest building are
metrics used to quantify some of the world's greatest architects.

Deceased Architect

Living Architect
(Aggregate Statistics)

Name	Age	Number of Projects	Fame (Average Google Searches)	Tallest Building (m)
Louis Sullivan	67	100	9900	73
Eliel Saarinen	76	30	2400	
Frank Lloyd Wright	91	532	135000	67
Walter Gropius	86	25	22200	246
Ludwig Mies van Der Rohe	83	39	74000	223
Le Corbusier	77	58	135000	154
Richard Neutra	78	81	8100	
Buckminster Fuller	87	11	33100	
Alvar Aalto	78	92	33100	
Hassan Fathy	89	112	2900	
Louis Kahn	73	29	22200	106
Luis Barragán	86	43	14800	
Philip Johnson	74	63	14800	275
Charles Eames	71	11	22200	
Oscar Niemeyer	104	600	60500	
Eero Saarinen	51	56	18100	155
Kenzo Tange	91	30	8100	243
I.M. Pei	97	70	18100	
Paul Rudolph	78	225	3600	
James Stirling	66	109	3600	
Alison Smithson	65	140	320	
Frank Gehry	85	66	60500	265
Peter Eisenman	81	46	12100	
Kisho Kurokawa	73	87	2400	
Michael Graves	79	134	14800	70
Richard Meier	79	144	22200	116
Norman Foster	79	268	12100	411
Glenn Murcutt	77	27	6600	
Renzo Piano	76	92	60500	310
Moshe Safdie	75	75	6600	
Lebbeus Woods	72	25	6600	
Toyo Ito	73	84	18100	113
Tadao Ando	72	156	40500	
Peter Zumthor	71	21	27100	
Thom Mayne	70	125	3600	300
Rem Koolhaas	69	274	33100	234
Samuel Mockbee	57	14	590	
Jean Nouvel	68	224	27100	380
Daniel Libeskind	68	55	27100	192
Steven Holl	66	146	18100	123
Jacques Herzog	64	430	1600	
Zaha Hadid	63	950	135000	
Kengo Kuma	60	145	14800	
Tom Kundig	59	158	2400	
Shigeru Ban	56	222	27100	
Greg Lynn	50	27	2900	
Joshua Prince-Ramus	44	33	1000	
Bjarke Ingels	39	170	14800	150

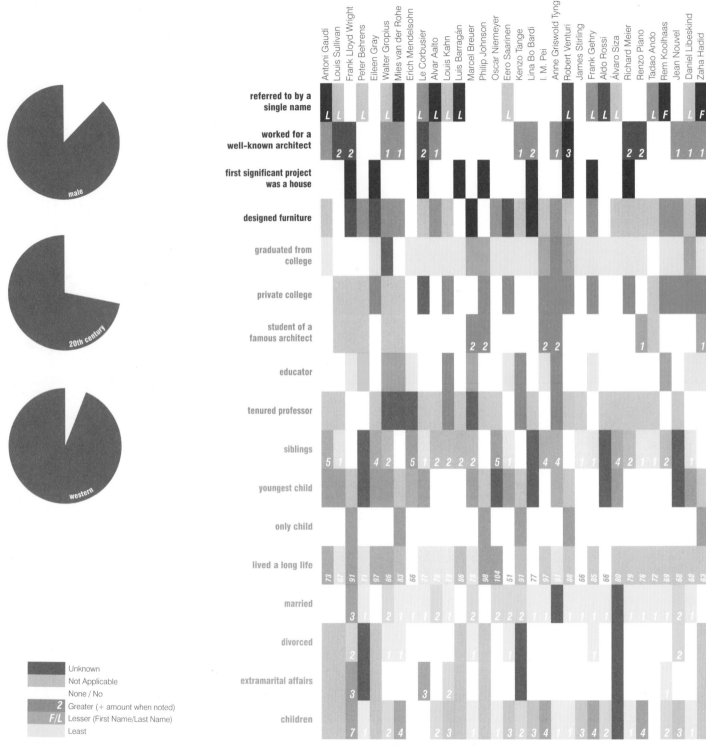

the architectural genome

What are the lifestyle characteristics of some of the world's great architects? This diagram charts personal characteristics to find similarities among these intriguing architectural figures.

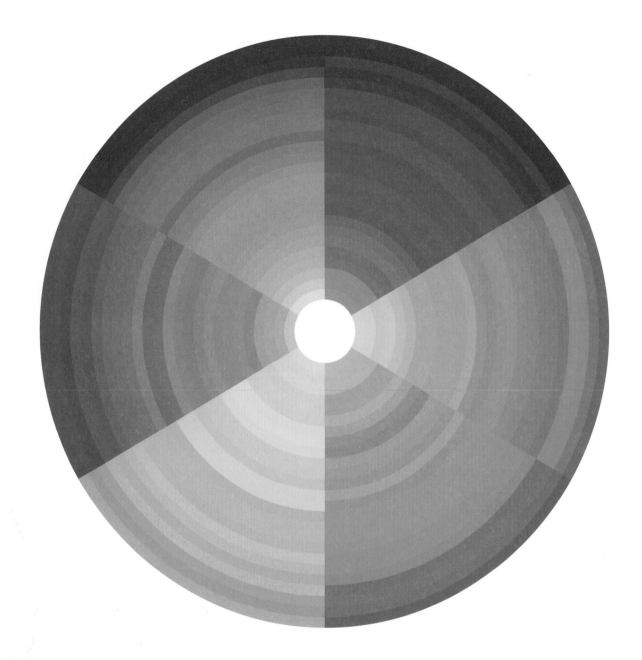

architectural color wheels

Architecture is colorful! The diagram above is a color wheel derived from an internet image search for buildings whose exterior surfaces are primary and secondary colors; each band representing a new image. The diagram on the right-hand page is constructed using well-known buildings that represent the rich colors of the color wheel.

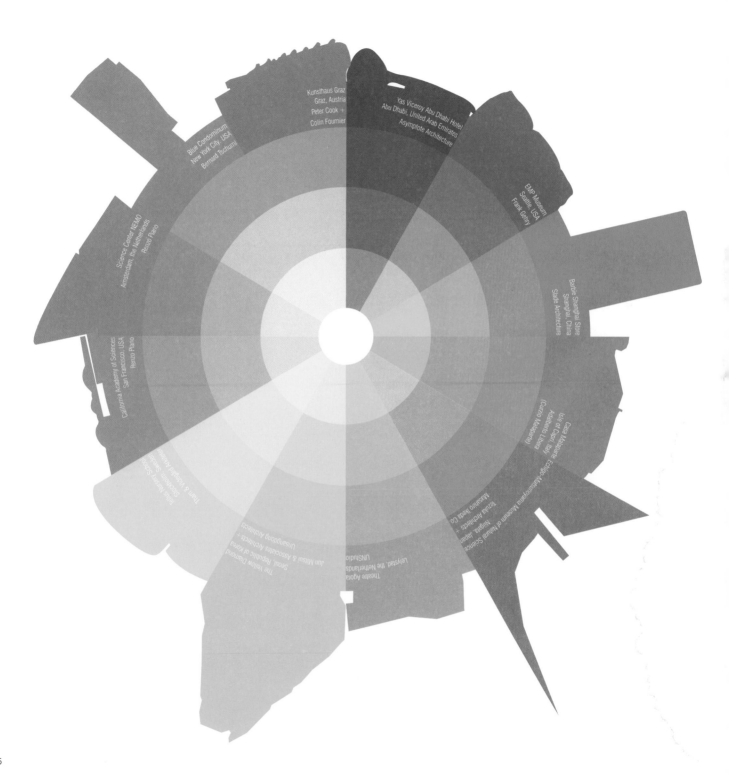

Kunsthaus Graz
Graz, Austria
Peter Cook +
Colin Fournier

Yas Viceroy Abu Dhabi Hotel
Abu Dhabi, United Arab Emirates
Asymptote Architecture

Blue Condominum
New York City, USA
Bernard Tschumi

EMP Museum
Seattle, USA
Frank Gehry

Science Center NEMO
Amsterdam, the Netherlands
Renzo Piano

Barbie Shanghai Store
Shanghai, China
Slade Architecture

California Academy of Sciences
San Francisco, USA
Renzo Piano

Casa Malaparte
Isle of Capri, Italy
Adalberto Libera
(Curzio Malaparte)

Tham & Videgård Arkitekter

Tellus Nursery School
Stockholm, Sweden

Jun Mitsui & Associates Architects +
Unsangdong Architects

The Yellow Diamond
Seoul, Republic of Korea

UNStudio

Theatre Agora
Lelystad, the Netherlands

Tezuka Architects Co.

Niigata, Japan
Matsunoyama Museum of Natural Science
Echigo-Matsunoyama Museum of Natural Science

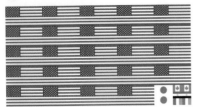

FRANK LLOYD WRIGHT
USA: 404	97.5%
Japan: 6	1.5%
Canada: 2	0.6%
Egypt: 1	0.2%
Ireland: 1	0.2%
TOTAL: 414	**100%**

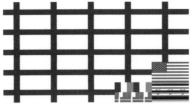

ALVAR AALTO
Finland: 76	87%
Croatia: 1	1%
Estonia:1	1%
USA: 4	5%
France: 2	2%
Italy: 1	1%
Iraq: 1	1%
Denmark: 1	1%
Germany: 1	1%
TOTAL: 88	**100%**

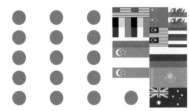

KISHO KUROKAWA
Japan: 34	63%
Bulgaria: 1	2%
Germany: 1	2%
Australia: 2	4%
China: 1	2%
USA: 1	2%
France:1	2%
Belgium: 1	2%
Singapore: 4	7%
Malaysia: 1	2%
Netherlands: 1	2%
Kazakhstan: 2	4%
Russia: 2	4%
Wales: 2	4%
TOTAL: 54	**100%**

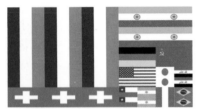

LE CORBUSIER
Switzerland: 7	12%
France: 28	48%
Germany: 2	4%
USSR: 2	4%
Chile: 1	2%
Brazil: 1	2%
Argentina: 1	2%
USA: 2	4%
India: 10	16%
Iraq: 1	2%
Japan: 1	2%
Italy: 1	2%
TOTAL: 57	**100%**

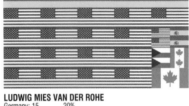

LUDWIG MIES VAN DER ROHE
Germany: 15	20%
Spain: 1	1%
Czech Republic: 1	1%
USA: 54	71%
Mexico: 1	1%
Canada: 4	6%
TOTAL: 76	**100%**

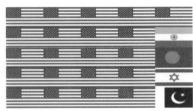

LOUIS KAHN
USA: 24	84%
India: 1	4%
Bangladesh: 1	4%
Pakistan: 1	4%
Israel: 1	4%
TOTAL: 28	**100%**

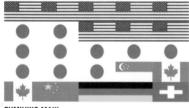

FUMIHIKO MAKI
USA: 8	34%
Japan: 9	38%
Germany: 2	8%
Canada: 2	8%
Taipei: 1	4%
Singapore: 1	4%
Switzerland: 1	4%
TOTAL: 24	**100%**

KENZO TANGE
Japan: 14	49%
Italy: 3	11%
Singapore: 5	19%
Yugoslavia:1	3%
USA: 1	3%
Bahrain: 1	3%
Algeria:1	3%
Vietnam: 1	3%
Nigeria:1	3%
Jordan:1	3%
TOTAL: 29	**100%**

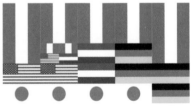

ALDO ROSSI
Italy: 7	50%
Japan: 2	16%
USA: 1	9%
Netherlands: 1	9%
Germany: 2	16%
TOTAL: 13	**100%**

who built where?

A representation of the predominance of work
in specific countries by each architect.

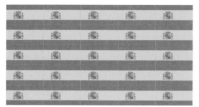

ANTONI GAUDÍ
SPAIN: 7	100%
TOTAL: 7	**100%**

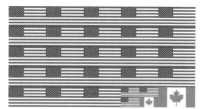

PHILIP JOHNSON
USA: 21	95%
Canada: 1	5%
TOTAL: 22	**100%**

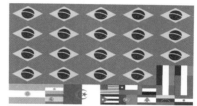

OSCAR NIEMEYER
Brazil: 70	76%
France: 3	3%
Italy: 3	3%
Argentina: 5	5%
Algeria: 4	4%
Venezuela: 1	1%
Lebanon: 1	1%
Portugal: 1	1%
UAE: 1	1%
Chile: 1	1%
Cuba: 1	1%
Paraguay: 1	1%
Spain: 1	1%
USA: 1	1%
TOTAL: 94	**100%**

VICTOR HORTA
Belgium: 42	98%
France: 1	2%
TOTAL: 43	**100%**

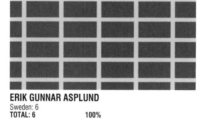

ERIK GUNNAR ASPLUND
Sweden: 6	100%
TOTAL: 6	**100%**

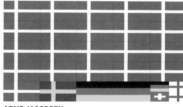

ARNE JACOBSEN
Denmark: 98	84%
Sweden: 4	4%
Germany: 10	9%
Switzerland: 1	1%
England: 2	2%
TOTAL: 115	**100%**

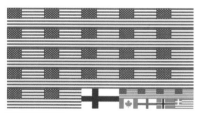

EERO SAARINEN
USA: 50	88%
Finland: 2	4%
England: 1	2%
Norway: 1	2%
Greece: 1	2%
Canada: 1	2%
TOTAL: 56	**100%**

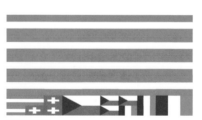

ADOLF LOOS
Switzerland: 1	3%
Czech Republic: 2	7%
Austria: 23	83%
France: 2	7%
TOTAL: 28	**100%**

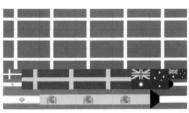

JØRN UTZON
Denmark: 11	61%
Sweden: 2	12%
Australia: 1	5%
Iran: 1	5%
Spain: 2	12%
Kuwait: 1	5%
TOTAL: 18	**100%**

Rafael Moneo chromachrono

Rafael Moneo (1958–present)
Selected works, 1967–2012.

Pamplona Bullring Extension, 1967
National Museum of Roman Art, 1985
San Pablo Airport Terminal, 1991
Atocha Station, 1992
Thyssen-Bornemisza Museum, 1992
Davis Museum & Cultural Center
Diagonal L'Illa Building, 1994
Museum of Modern Art in Stockholm, 1998
Kursaal Palace, 1999
Casa de Cultura, 1997
Murcia Town Hall, 1998
L'Audition, 1999
Audrey Jones Beck Building, 2000
Cathedral of Our Lady of the Angels, 2002
Studio Addition for Cranbrook Academy of Art, 2002
Arenberg Campus Library, 2002
Valladolid Science Museum, 2003
Royal Archive of Navarre, 2003
Julián Chivite Winery 2002
Gregorio Marañón Maternity & Pediatric Hospital, 2003
Beulas Foundation, 2006
Prado Museum Extension, 2007
Chase Center RISD Museum of Art, 2008
Library at University of Deusto, 2009
Palacio de Congresos de Toledo, 2009
Beirut Souks, 2010
Building Aragonia, 2010
Baltasar Lobo Museum, 2010
Grand Hyatt Hotel & Office, 2012
Iglesia de Iesu San Sebastián, 2011

MVRDV chromachrono — Selected works, 1996–2013.

Top labels (left to right):
- Otterlo Lodge, 1996
- Villa VPRO, 1997
- Wozoco, 1997
- Borneo 18, 1999
- Calveen Office Building, 1999
- Netherlands Pavilion, EXPO 2000, 2000
- Tarra Tower, 2002
- Silodam, 2003
- UPV Munich, 2003
- Lloyd Hotel, 2004
- Matsudai Center, 2004
- De Effenaar, 2005
- Water Villas, 2005
- Frosilos, 2005
- Barcode House, 2005
- Cancer Center, Amsterdam, 2005
- Mirador, 2005
- Parkrand, 2006
- Didden Village, 2006
- Gyre, 2007
- Westerdok, 2009
- Celosia, 2009
- Why Factory, 2009
- Le Monolithe, 2010
- Balancing Barn, 2010
- DNB Headquarters, 2012
- Teletech Call Center, 2012
- Book Mountain, 2012
- Glass Farm, 2013
- Chungha Building, 2013

Bottom labels (left to right):
- Arnhem Lodge, 1996
- Hoenderloo Lodge, 1996
- NTR Headquarters, 1997
- Borneo 12, 1999
- Studio Thonik, 2001
- New Manor, 2004
- Haus Am Hang, 2005
- Anyang Peak, 2006

MVRDV chromachrono

Winy Maas, Jacob van Rijs, & Nathalie de Vries (1993–present)
Selected works, 1996–2013.

Multimedia Studio, 1996
M House, 1997
Weekend House, 1998
Small House, 2000
Gifu Kitagata Apartments, 2000

Issey Miyake Store, 2003
Dior Omotesando Store, 2003

21st Century Museum of Contemporary Art, 2004

Moriyama House, 2005

De Kunstline Theater & Cultural Center, 2006

Glass Pavilion at Toledo Museum of Art, 2006

Zollverein School of Management and Design, 2006
Naoshima Ferry Terminal, 2006
House A, 2006

Fabrikstrasse 4, Novartis Campus, 2006

Factory Building on Vitra Campus, 2007

New Museum of Contemporary Art, New York, 2007

Okurayama Apartments, 2008

Towada Arts Center, 2008

Serpentine Gallery Pavilion, 2009
Carina Shop, 2009

Rolex Learning Center, 2010

Teshima Art Museum, 2010
A Art House, 2010
Shakujii Apartments, 2011
Hiroshi Senju Museum Karuizawa, 2011
Shibaura House, 2011

Louvre-Lens, 2012

Tsuchihashi House, 2012
Fukita Pavilion, 2013

S House, 1996
Koga Park Café, 1998
O Museum, 1999

House in Plum Grove, 2003

Onishi Town Hall, 2005

Dentist Office, 2006

Seijo Townhouses, 2008

Derek Lam Store, 2009

C-Art House, 2010
Kumamoto Station, 2011
Garden & House, 2011

Juriko Fukutake Hall, Okayama University, 2013
Fukita Pavilion, 2013

SANAA chromachrono

Kazuyo Sejima & Ryue Nishizawa (1995–present)
Selected works, 1996–2013.

New York City Facts

Geography

Coordinates	40°42′N 74°00′W
Elevation	33ft (10m)

(2013)

Population

Total	8,405,837
Metro	19,949,502
Density	27,778.7 people/mi² (10,725.4 people/km²)

Area

Total	468.9mi² (1,214.4km²)
Land	304.8mi² (789.4km²)
Water	164.1mi² (425km²)
Metro	13,318mi² (34,493km²)
Parkland	42.5mi² (110km²)

Climate

av. min-max temperature 47.9–62.0°F (8.8–16.6°C)

av. rainfall 49.9in (126.75cm)

History

settled as New Amsterdam 1625

Robert Moses influences NYC urban planning 1920–60

crime rate drops dramatically 1990s

NEW YORK CITY, US

London Facts

Geography

Coordinates	51°30′N 0°7′W
Elevation	79ft (24.1m)

(2012)

Population

City	8,308,369
Urban	9,787,426
Metro	15,010,295
Density	13,690 people/mi² (36,457 people/km²)

Area

City	606.95mi² (1,572km²)
Urban	671mi² (1,737.9km²)
Metro	3,236.31mi² (8,382km²)
Parkland	54.7mi² (141.67km²)

Climate

av. min-max temperature 45.5–59.4°F (7.5–15.2°C)

av. rainfall 24in (61cm)

History

settled by Romans 43 CE

world's largest city 1831–1925

bombed for eight months (The Blitz) 1940–41

LONDON, UK

Dubai Facts

Geography

Coordinates	25°15′N 55°18′E
Elevation	52ft (15.8m)

(2013)

Population

Total	2,106,177
Density	1,199.6 people/mi^2 (463.2 people/km^2)

Area

Total	1,588mi^2 (14,112.9km^2)
Green Space	24.6372mi^2 (163.81km^2)

Climate

av. min-max temperature	72.1–92.1°F (22.3–33.4°C)
av. rainfall	3.71in (9.4cm)

History

settled	1799
population tripled	1968–75

Economy

real estate and construction (22.6%)	entrepôt (15%)
trade (16%)	financial services (11%)

DUBAI, UAE

Tokyo Facts

Geography

Coordinates	35°41′N 139°41′E
Elevation	131ft (40m)

(2011)

Population

Total	13,185,502
Metro	35,682,460
Density	16,000 people/mi^2 (6.177.6/km^2)

Area

City	844.66mi^2 (2,1187km^2)
Metro	5,240mi^2 (13,572km^2)
Parkland	197.945mi^2 (512.68km^2)

Climate

av. min-max temperature 55.3–67.9°F (12.9–19.4°C)

av. rainfall 60.2in (153cm)

History

fishing village Edo grows to one million 18th century

city of Tokyo established 1896

half the city destroyed in bombing 1944

Economy	Tourism
largest metropolitan economy worldwide	4.81 million foreign visits
Tokyo urban area GDP is US$2.91 trillion	420 million Japanese visits

TOKYO, JAPAN

dot-to-dot location of architecture schools

Like children at play, we've connected the historic dots of architectural education.

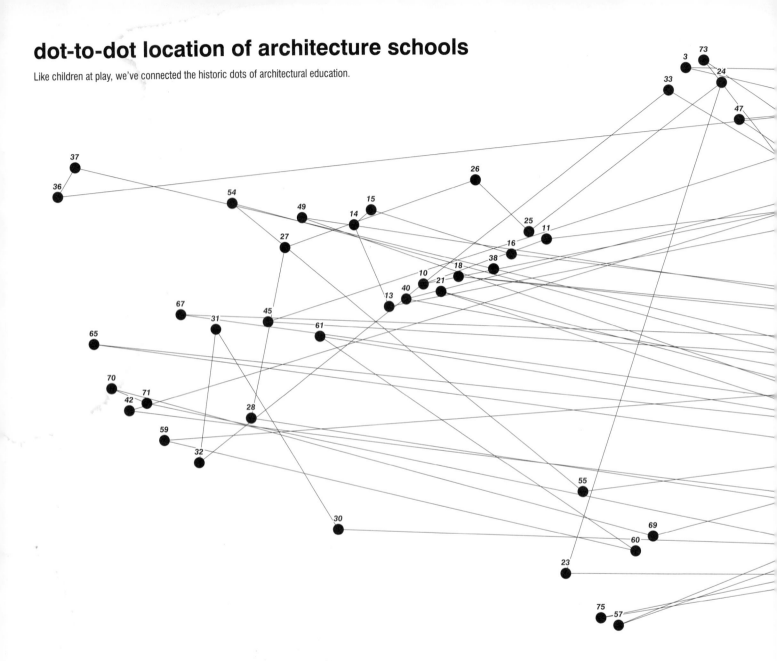

1 École nationale supérieure des Beaux-Arts, Paris	11 Massachusetts Institute of Technology	21 Pratt Institute	31 Washington University in St Louis
2 Royal Danish Academy of Fine Arts	12 Polytechnic University of Milan	22 Sydney Technical College	32 Rice University
3 Glasgow School of Art	13 University of Pennsylvania	23 University of Chile	33 University College Dublin
4 Vienna University of Technology	14 Cornell University	24 University of Liverpool	34 Technion Israel Institute of Technology
5 The Bartlett, University College London	15 Syracuse University	25 Harvard Graduate School of Design	35 University of Cambridge
6 Technical University Delft	16 Rhode Island School of Design	26 University of Michigan	36 University of Oregon
7 Architectural Association School of Architecture	17 University of Tokyo	27 University of Michigan	37 University of Washington
8 Helsinki University of Technology	18 Columbia University	28 Auburn University	38 Yale School of Architecture
9 ETH Zurich	19 Tokyo Institute of Technology	29 University of Witwatersrand	39 American University of Cairo
10 Cooper Union	20 Royal Melbourne Institute of Technology	30 National University of Engineering Peru	40 Princeton University

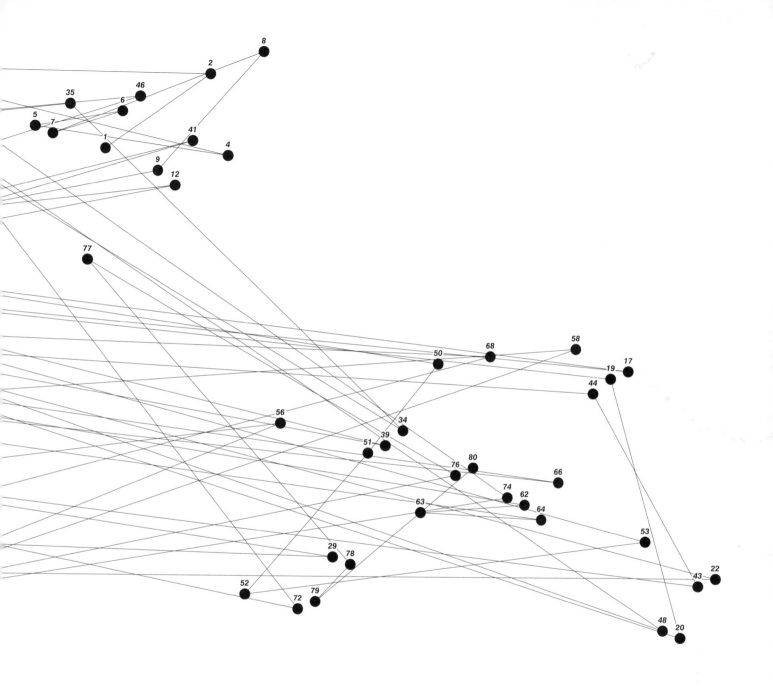

41 Bauhaus
42 University of Southern California
43 University of Sydney
44 Kyoto University
45 University of Cincinnati
46 Gerrit Rietveld Academie
47 Oxford Brooks University
48 University of Melbourne
49 Cranbrook Academy of Art
50 University of Tehran

51 Cairo University
52 The University of Cape Town
53 University of Queensland
54 Taliesin
55 University City of Caracas
56 Alexandria University
57 University of Buenos Aires
58 Kyung Hee University
59 University of Texas at Austin
60 Mackenzie Presbyterian University

61 University of Virginia
62 University of Technology Malaysia
63 University of Nairobi
64 National University of Singapore
65 University of California, Berkeley
66 Chinese University of Hong Kong
67 Kansas State University
68 Virginia Polytechnic Institute
69 Federal University of Rio de Janeiro
70 California Polytechnic State University

71 Southern California Institute of Architecture
72 Nelson Mandela Metropolitan University
73 University of Edinburgh
74 Torcuato di Tella University
75 Limkokwing University of Creative Technology
76 American University of Sharjah
77 Institute for Advanced Architecture of Catalonia
78 University of Kwazulu-Natal
79 Nelson Mandela Metropolitan University
80 School of Planning and Architecture

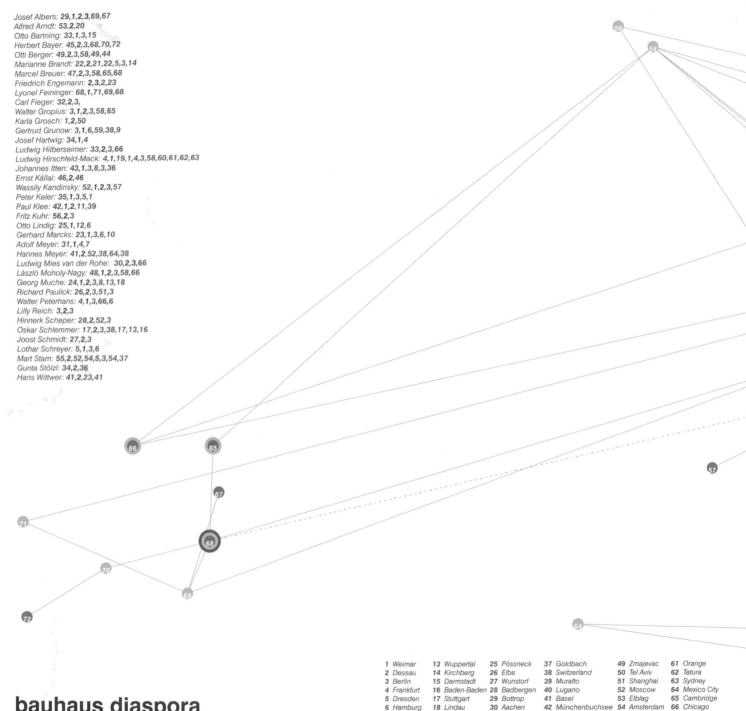

Josef Albers: **29,1,2,3,69,67**
Alfred Arndt: **53,2,20**
Otto Bartning: **33,1,3,15**
Herbert Bayer: **45,2,3,68,70,72**
Otti Berger: **49,2,3,58,49,44**
Marianne Brandt: **22,2,21,22,5,3,14**
Marcel Breuer: **47,2,3,58,65,68**
Friedrich Engemann: **2,3,2,23**
Lyonel Feininger: **68,1,71,69,68**
Carl Fieger: **32,2,3,**
Walter Gropius: **3,1,2,3,58,65**
Karla Grosch: **1,2,50**
Gertrud Grunow: **3,1,6,59,38,9**
Josef Hartwig: **34,1,4**
Ludwig Hilberseimer: **33,2,3,66**
Ludwig Hirschfeld-Mack: **4,1,19,1,4,3,58,60,61,62,63**
Johannes Itten: **43,1,3,8,3,36**
Ernst Kállai: **46,2,46**
Wassily Kandinsky: **52,1,2,3,57**
Peter Keler: **35,1,3,5,1**
Paul Klee: **42,1,2,11,39**
Fritz Kuhr: **56,2,3**
Otto Lindig: **25,1,12,6**
Gerhard Marcks: **23,1,3,6,10**
Adolf Meyer: **31,1,4,7**
Hannes Meyer: **41,2,52,38,64,38**
Ludwig Mies van der Rohe: **30,2,3,66**
László Moholy-Nagy: **48,1,2,3,58,66**
Georg Muche: **24,1,2,3,8,13,18**
Richard Paulick: **26,2,3,51,3**
Walter Peterhans: **4,1,3,66,6**
Lilly Reich: **3,2,3**
Hinnerk Scheper: **28,2,52,3**
Oskar Schlemmer: **17,2,3,38,17,13,16**
Joost Schmidt: **27,2,3**
Lothar Schreyer: **5,1,3,6**
Mart Stam: **55,2,52,54,5,3,54,37**
Gunta Stölzl: **34,2,36**
Hans Wittwer: **41,2,23,41**

bauhaus diaspora

Mapping the migration of many of the faculty and students
of one of the most famous architecture schools in history.

1 Weimar	13 Wuppertal	25 Pössneck	37 Goldbach	49 Zmajevac	61 Orange
2 Dessau	14 Kirchberg	26 Elbe	38 Switzerland	50 Tel Aviv	62 Tatura
3 Berlin	15 Darmstadt	27 Wunstorf	39 Muralto	51 Shanghai	63 Sydney
4 Frankfurt	16 Baden-Baden	28 Badbergen	40 Lugano	52 Moscow	64 Mexico City
5 Dresden	17 Stuttgart	29 Bottrop	41 Basel	53 Elblag	65 Cambridge
6 Hamburg	18 Lindau	30 Aachen	42 Münchenbuchsee	54 Amsterdam	66 Chicago
7 Baltrum	19 Wackersdorf	31 Mechernich	43 Suderen-Linden	55 Purmerend	67 New Haven
8 Krefeld	20 Probstzella	32 Mainz	44 Auschwitz	56 Liège	68 New York City
9 Leverkusen	21 Gotha	33 Karlsruhe	45 Haag	57 Paris	69 Ashville
10 Cologne	22 Chemnitz	34 Munich	46 Budapest	58 London	70 Aspen
11 Düsseldorf	23 Halle	35 Kiel	47 Pécs	59 England	71 Oakland
12 Dornburg	24 Querfurt	36 Zurich	48 Bácsborsód	60 Hay	72 Los Angeles

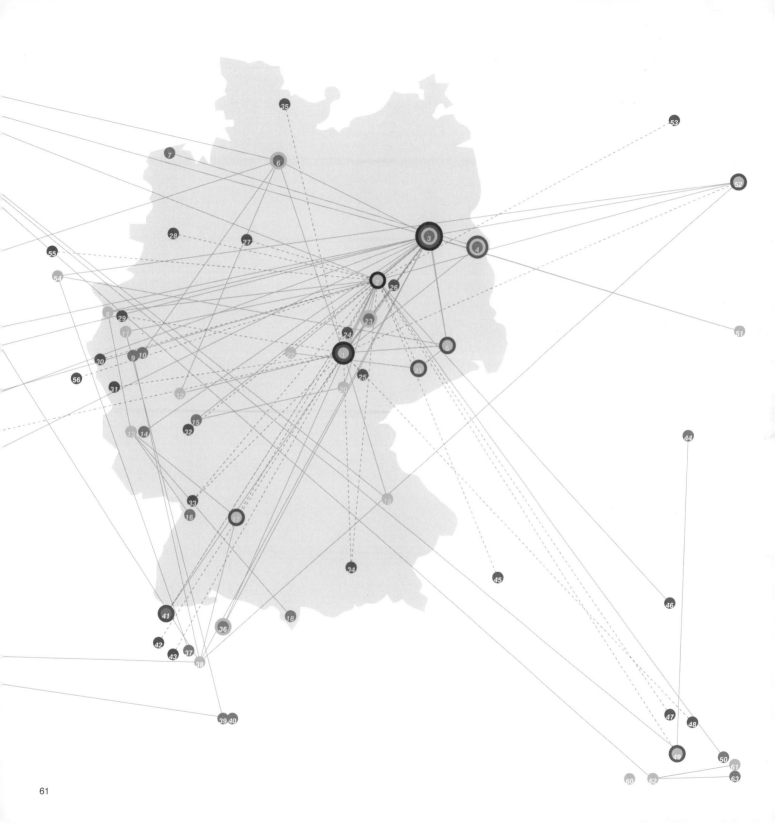

big builder, big data

A comparison of the number of Google hits that an architect currently receives on the left-hand page is compared to the approximate number of projects they have completed on the right-hand page.

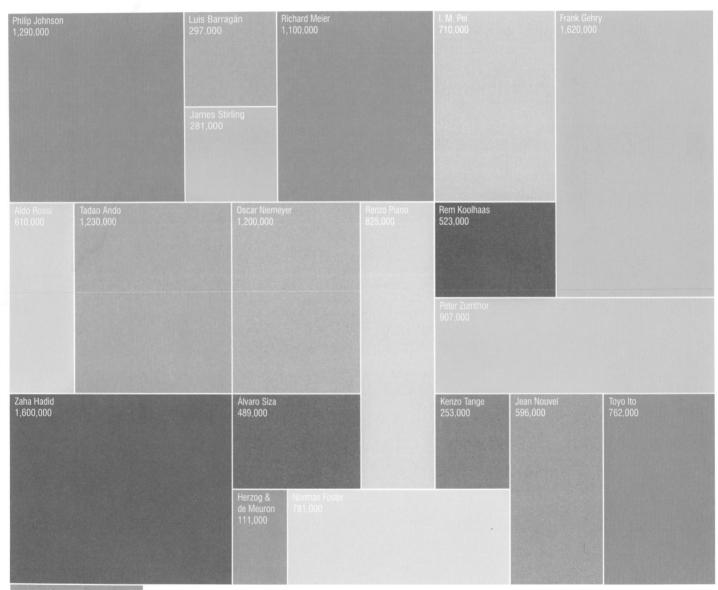

Philip Johnson
1,290,000

Luis Barragán
297,000

Richard Meier
1,100,000

I. M. Pei
710,000

Frank Gehry
1,620,000

James Stirling
281,000

Aldo Rossi
610,000

Tadao Ando
1,230,000

Oscar Niemeyer
1,200,000

Renzo Piano
825,000

Rem Koolhaas
523,000

Peter Zumthor
907,000

Zaha Hadid
1,600,000

Álvaro Siza
489,000

Kenzo Tange
253,000

Jean Nouvel
596,000

Toyo Ito
762,000

Herzog & de Meuron
111,000

Norman Foster
781,000

Google Hits

Philip Johnson
160

Luis Barragán
102

James Stirling
103

Richard Meier
95

I. M. Pei
212

Frank Gehry
243

Renzo Piano
76

Kenzo Tange
255

Aldo Rossi
292

Tadao Ando
154

Oscar Niemeyer
500

Rem Koolhaas
107

Norman Foster
250

Álvaro Siza
172

Jean Nouvel
85

Zaha Hadid
85

Herzog & de Meuron
128

Peter Zumthor
43

Toyo Ito
85

Completed Works

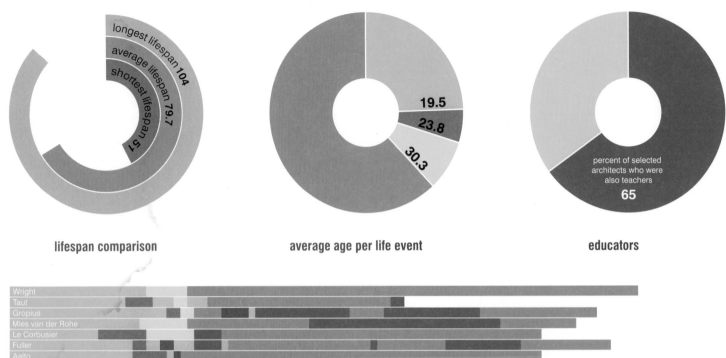

lifespan comparison

longest lifespan **104**
average lifespan **79.7**
shortest lifespan **51**

19.5
23.8
30.3

average age per life event

percent of selected architects who were also teachers
65

educators

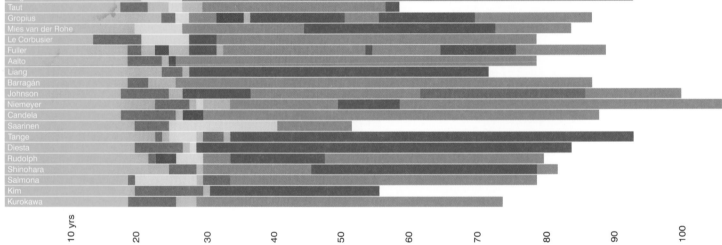

Wright
Taut
Gropius
Mies van der Rohe
Le Corbusier
Fuller
Aalto
Liang
Barragán
Johnson
Niemeyer
Candela
Saarinen
Tange
Diesta
Rudolph
Shinohara
Salmona
Kim
Kurokawa

10 yrs | 20 | 30 | 40 | 50 | 60 | 70 | 80 | 90 | 100

tracking age specific events

career track

This and the following two spreads track significant moments in the
lives of well-respected architects. When did these architects begin
their practice? When did they win their first major awards? When
were they married or divorced? These diagrams treat life
as a running track that answers these compelling questions.

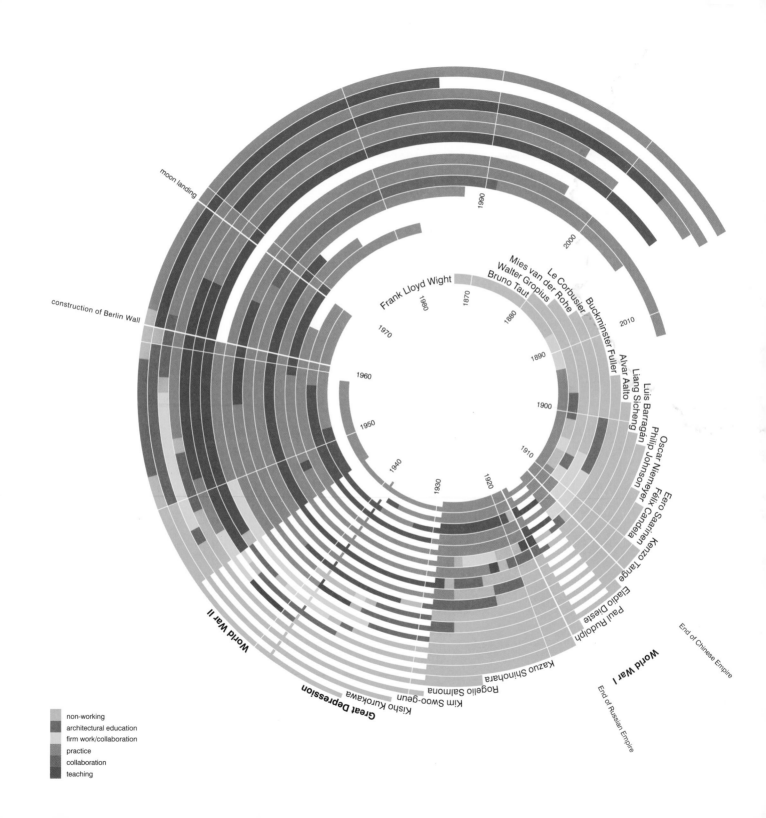

moon landing

construction of Berlin Wall

World War II

Great Depression

Kisho Kurokawa

Kim Swoo-geun

Rogelio Salmona

Kazuo Shinohara

World War I

End of Russian Empire

End of Chinese Empire

Paul Rudolph

Eladio Dieste

Kenzo Tange

Félix Candela

Eero Saarinen

Philip Johnson

Oscar Niemeyer

Luis Barragán

Liang Sicheng

Alvar Aalto

Buckminster Fuller

Le Corbusier

Mies van der Rohe

Walter Gropius

Bruno Taut

Frank Lloyd Wight

1870
1880
1890
1900
1910
1920
1930
1940
1950
1960
1970
1980
1990
2000
2010

- non-working
- architectural education
- firm work/collaboration
- practice
- collaboration
- teaching

Europe

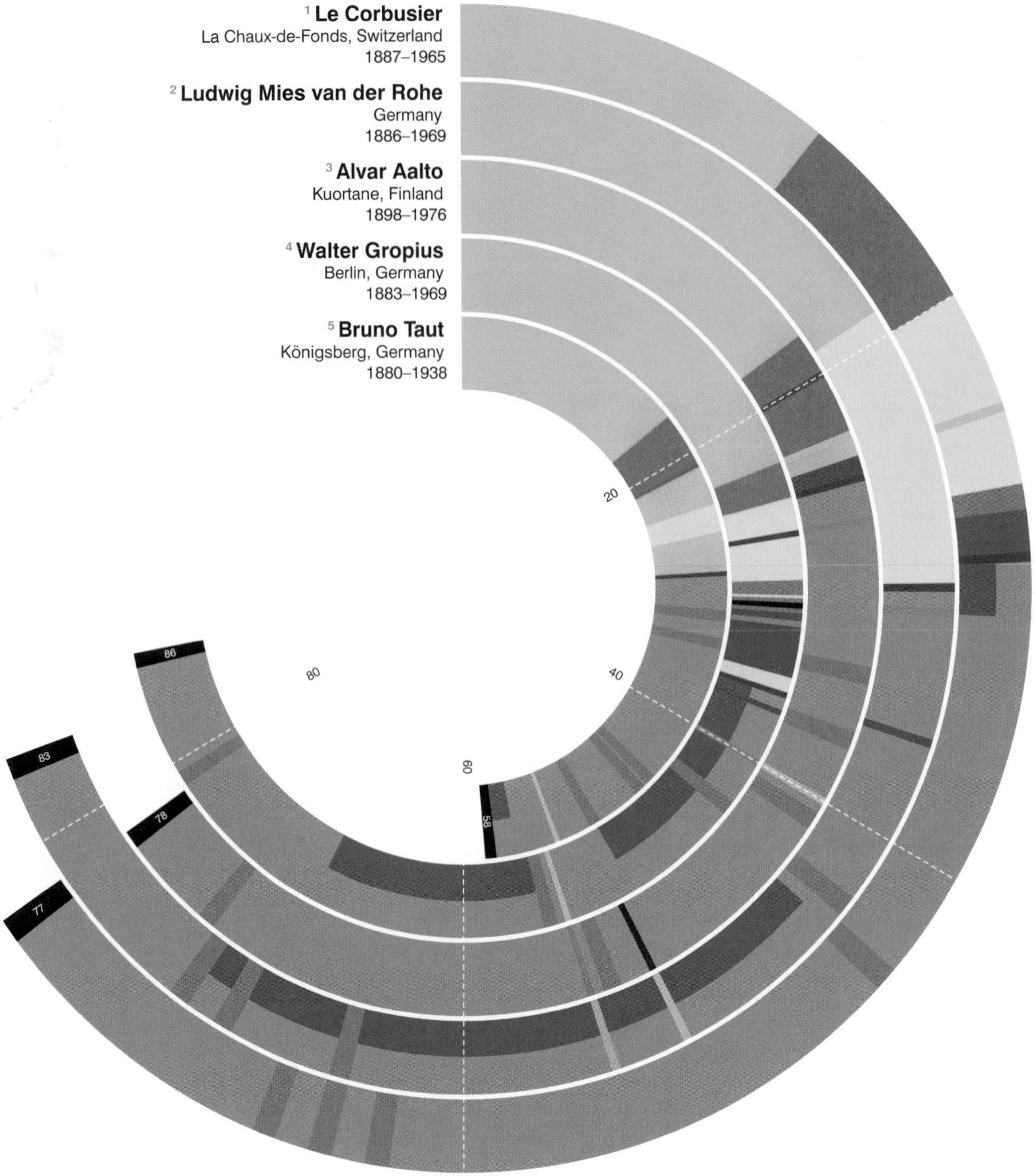

[1] **Le Corbusier**
La Chaux-de-Fonds, Switzerland
1887–1965

[2] **Ludwig Mies van der Rohe**
Germany
1886–1969

[3] **Alvar Aalto**
Kuortane, Finland
1898–1976

[4] **Walter Gropius**
Berlin, Germany
1883–1969

[5] **Bruno Taut**
Königsberg, Germany
1880–1938

Asia

6 **Kenzo Tange**
Osaka, Japan
1913–2005

7 **Kisho Kurokawa**
Kanie, Aichi Prefecture, Japan
1934–2007

8 **Kazuo Shinohara**
Shizuoka, Japan
1925–2006

9 **Liang Sicheng**
Tokyo, Japan
1901–1972

10 **Kim Swoo-geun**
Chongjin, North Korea
1931–1986

non-working
architectural education
graduated
military service
firm work/collaboration
marriage
relationship
divorce
spouse's death
beginning own practice
practice
major projects
teaching
travel
major international award
death

North America

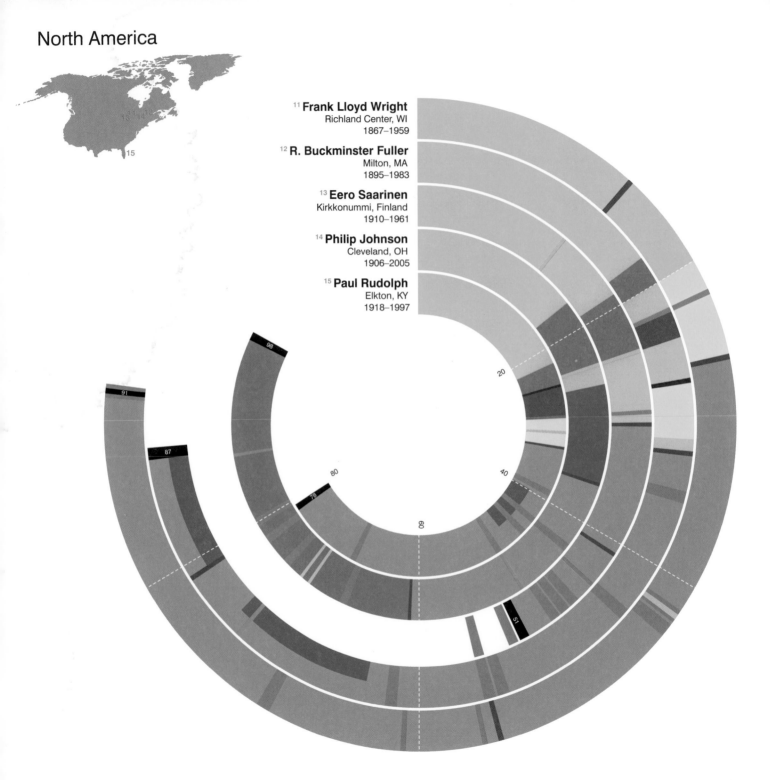

11 Frank Lloyd Wright
Richland Center, WI
1867–1959

12 R. Buckminster Fuller
Milton, MA
1895–1983

13 Eero Saarinen
Kirkkonummi, Finland
1910–1961

14 Philip Johnson
Cleveland, OH
1906–2005

15 Paul Rudolph
Elkton, KY
1918–1997

Latin America

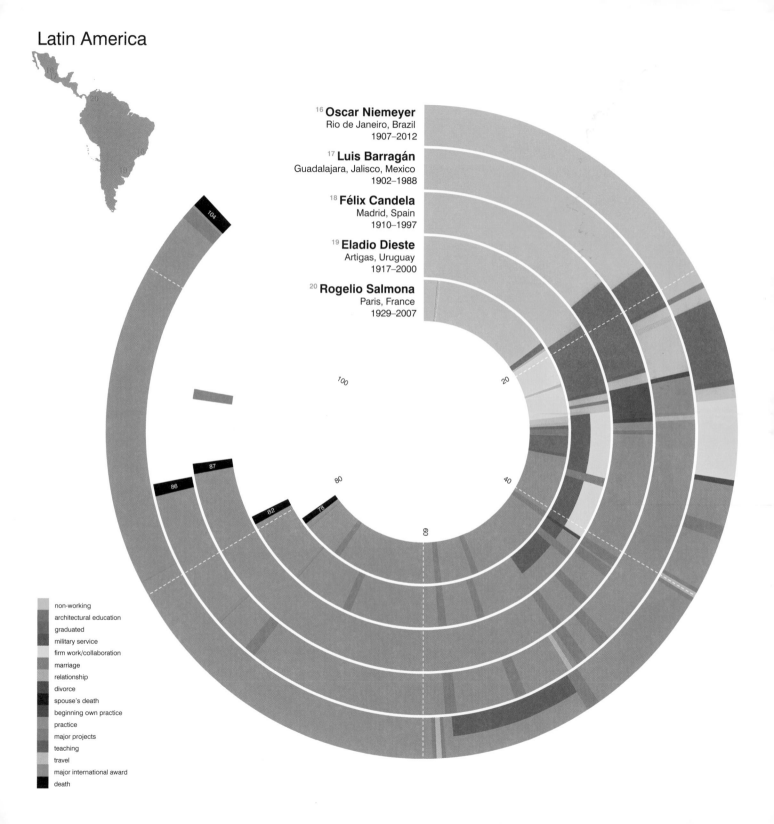

16 Oscar Niemeyer
Rio de Janeiro, Brazil
1907–2012

17 Luis Barragán
Guadalajara, Jalisco, Mexico
1902–1988

18 Félix Candela
Madrid, Spain
1910–1997

19 Eladio Dieste
Artigas, Uruguay
1917–2000

20 Rogelio Salmona
Paris, France
1929–2007

104

87

86

82

78

100

80

20

40

60

non-working
architectural education
graduated
military service
firm work/collaboration
marriage
relationship
divorce
spouse's death
beginning own practice
practice
major projects
teaching
travel
major international award
death

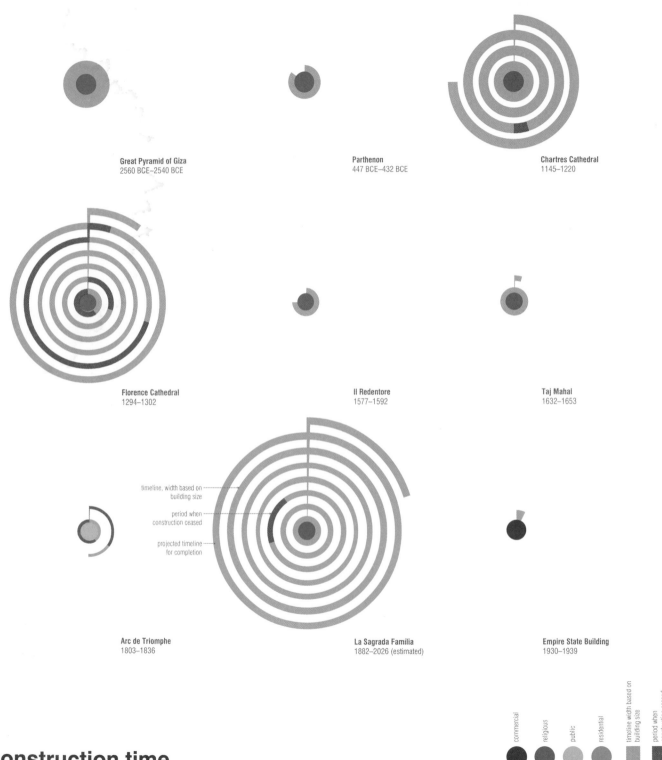

Great Pyramid of Giza
2560 BCE–2540 BCE

Parthenon
447 BCE–432 BCE

Chartres Cathedral
1145–1220

Florence Cathedral
1294–1302

Il Redentore
1577–1592

Taj Mahal
1632–1653

timeline, width based on
building size

period when
construction ceased

projected timeline
for completion

Arc de Triomphe
1803–1836

La Sagrada Familia
1882–2026 (estimated)

Empire State Building
1930–1939

commercial

religious

public

residential

timeline width based on
building size

period when
construction ceased

projected timeline
for completion

construction time

Lake Shore Drive Apartments
1949–1952

Brasília Cathedral
1958–1970

Sydney Opera House
1959–1973

Saint Pierre, Firminy
1970–2006

Seattle Central Library
1999–2004

30 St Mary Axe
2001–2003

Ningbo History Museum
2003–2008

Burj Khalifa
2004–2010

Sky City
90 days (estimated)

A comparison of a building's size with the length of time taken for its construction.

the distinguishing features game

Try to guess the architect by their distinguishing features – answers at bottom of page.

Frank Lloyd Wright
Ludwig Mies van der Rohe
Le Corbusier

Toyo Ito
Louis Kahn
Frank Gehry

E. Fay Jones
Renzo Piano
Alvaro Siza

Tadao Ando
Bjarke Ingels
Zaha Hadid

Rem Koolhaas
Alvar Aalto
Jean Nouvel

Moshe Safdie
Shigeru Ban
Oscar Niemeyer

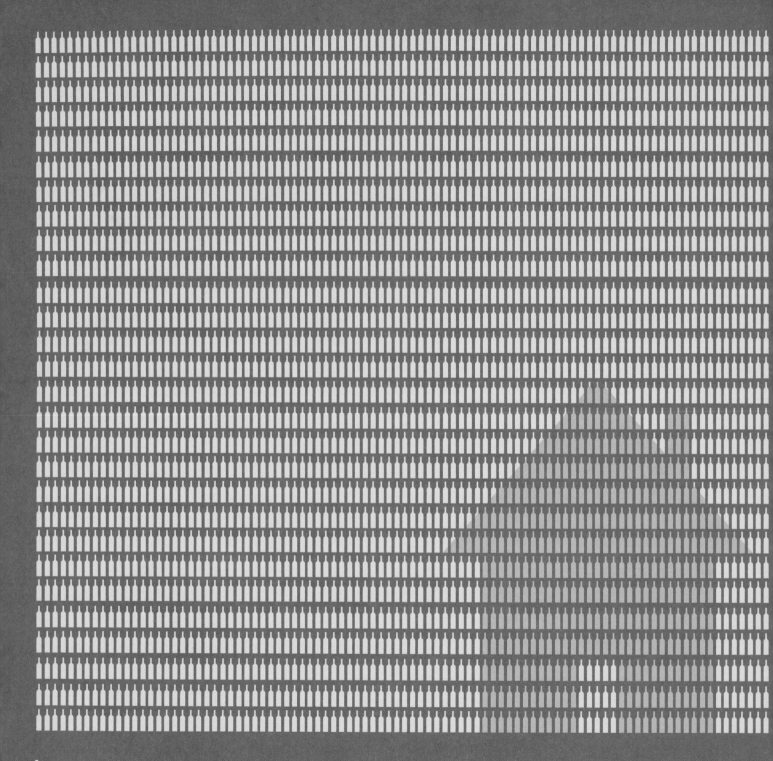

bottoms up

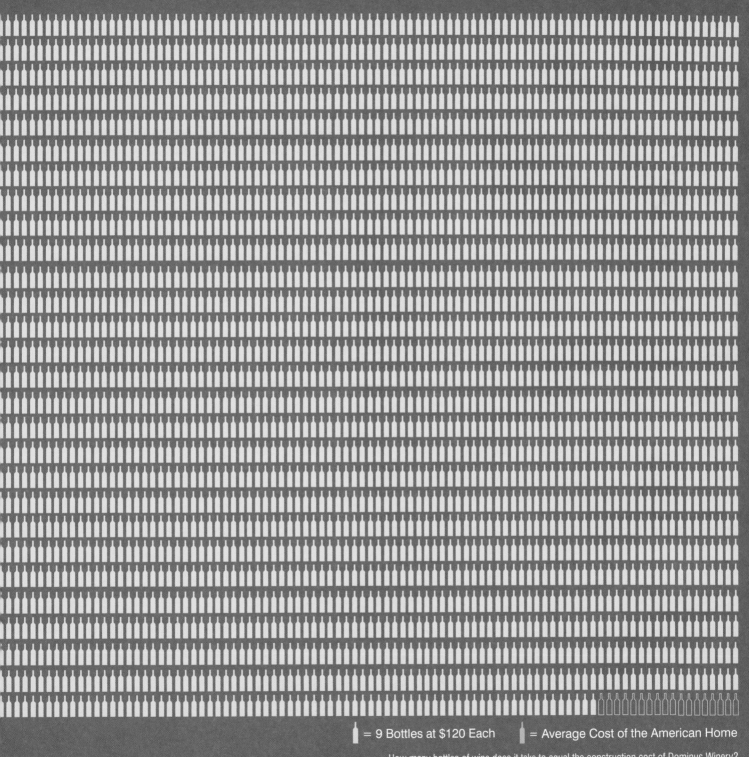

= 9 Bottles at $120 Each   = Average Cost of the American Home

How many bottles of wine does it take to equal the construction cost of Dominus Winery?

Aluminum House, 1971
House in Sakurajosui, 1975
Hotel D, 1977
House in Denenchofu, 1983
M Building in Kanda, 1986
Restaurant Pastina, 1989
Yatsushiro Municipal Museum, 1991
Hotel P, 1992
Old People's House in Yatsushiro, 1994
Nagaoka Lyric Hall, 1996
Agricultural Park Ota, 2000
W House in Inagi, 2002
Motomachi Chukagai Station, 2003
TOD'S Omotesando Building, 2004
Za-Koenji Public Theatre, 2009
Torres Porta Fira, 2010
Belle Vue Residences, 2010
Tokyo Mother's Clinic, 2011

Cottage in Sengataki, 1974
White U, 1976
House in Hamakoganei, 1983
House in Magomezawa, 1986
Guest House for Sapporo, 1989
T Building in Nakameguro, 1990
Public Kindergarten in Eckenheim, 1993
Serpentine Gallery Pavilion, 2002

Toyo Ito & Associates chromachrono

Toyo Ito (1971–present)
Selected works, 1971–2011.

UNStudio chromachrono

Ben van Berkel & Caroline Bos (1988–present)
Selected works, 1992–2013.

Karbouw, 1992
Erasmus Bridge, 1996
Vroom & Dreesmann department store, 1996
Bascule Bridgemaster's House, 1998
Het Valkhof Museum, 1998
Möbius House, 1998
NMR Facility, 2000
La Tour, 2000
Water Villas, 2001
Electrical Substation, 2002
Arnhem Central Bus Terminal, 2002

Villa Wilbrink

Waste Disposal Installation, 2000

IJsselstein Town Hall & Theatre, 2000
Living Tomorrow, 2002

Arnhem Central Car Park, 2002

Hotel Castell & Hamam, 2004
Galleria Department Store façade, 2004

La Defense Offices, 2004

Park & Rijn Towers, 2005
Villa NM, 2006

Mercedes-Benz Museum, 2006

Ardmore Residence, 2006

Theatre Agora, 2007
Music Theatre, 2008
Research Laboratory, 2008

Star Place façade, 2008

UN Studio Tower, 2010

Galleria Centercity façade, 2010

Education Executive Agency & Tax Offices, 2011

Arnhem Central Platform Roofs, 2011
Centre for Virtual Engineering, 2012

Mirai House, 2012

Hanjie Wanda Square, 2013

Kutaisi International Airport, 2013

covered up – '80s

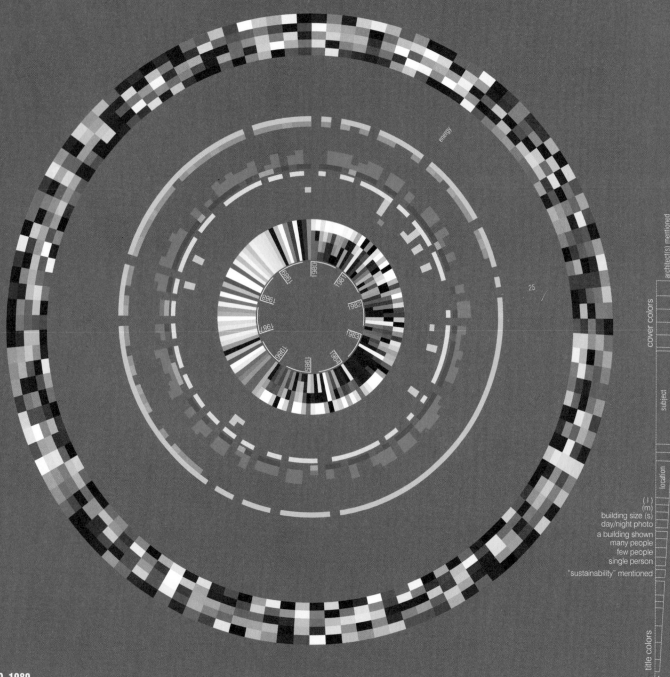

energy

25

1980
1981
1982
1983
1984
1985
1986
1987
1988
1989

architect(s) mentioned

cover colors

subject

location

(l)
(m)
building size (s)
day/night photo
a building shown
many people
few people
single person

"sustainability" mentioned

title colors

year

1980–1989
Architecture Magazine

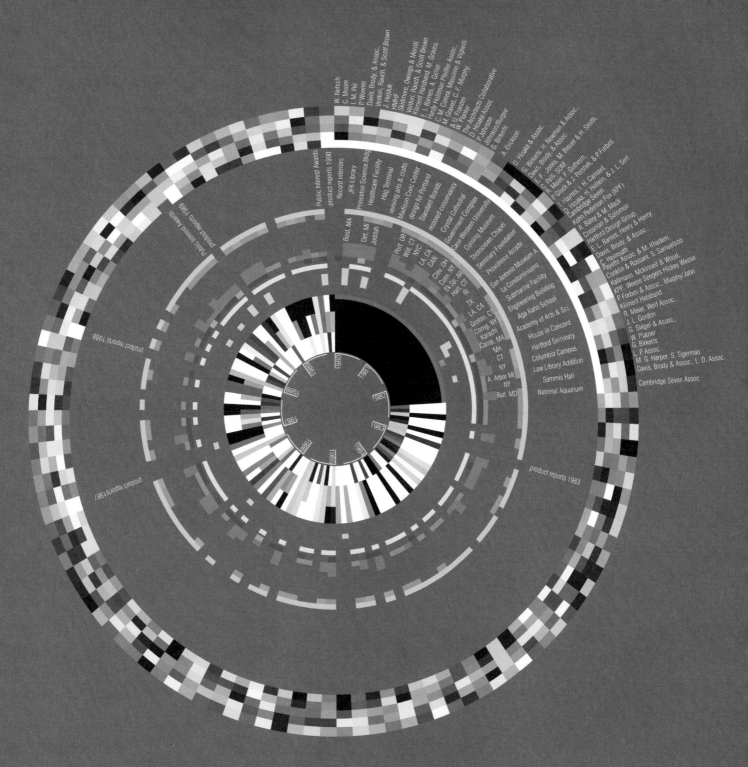

1980–1989
Architectural Record

Dissecting color, text, and embedded content within the covers of two major architectural publications.

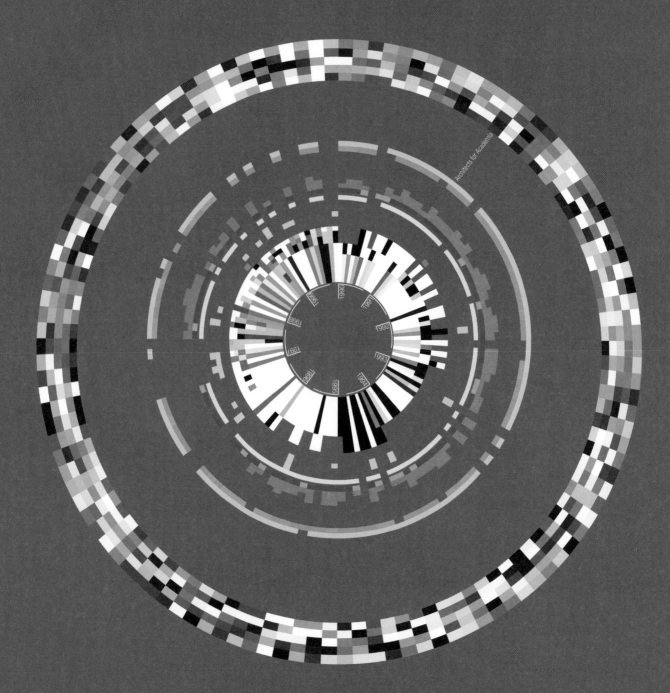

1990–1999
Architecture Magazine

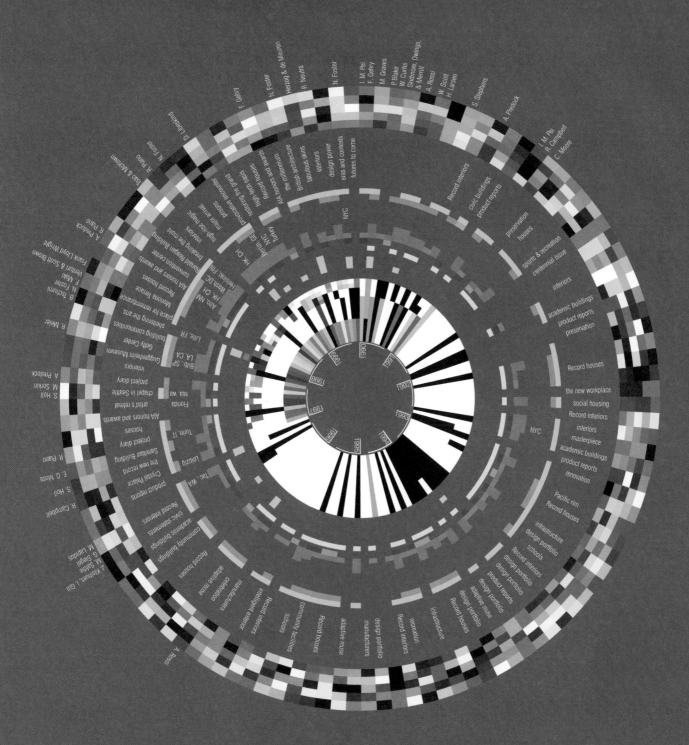

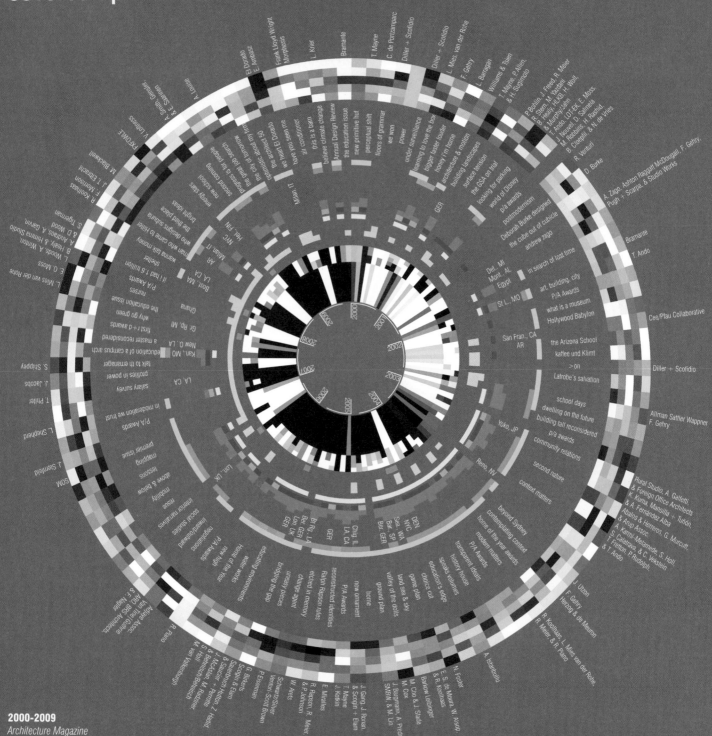

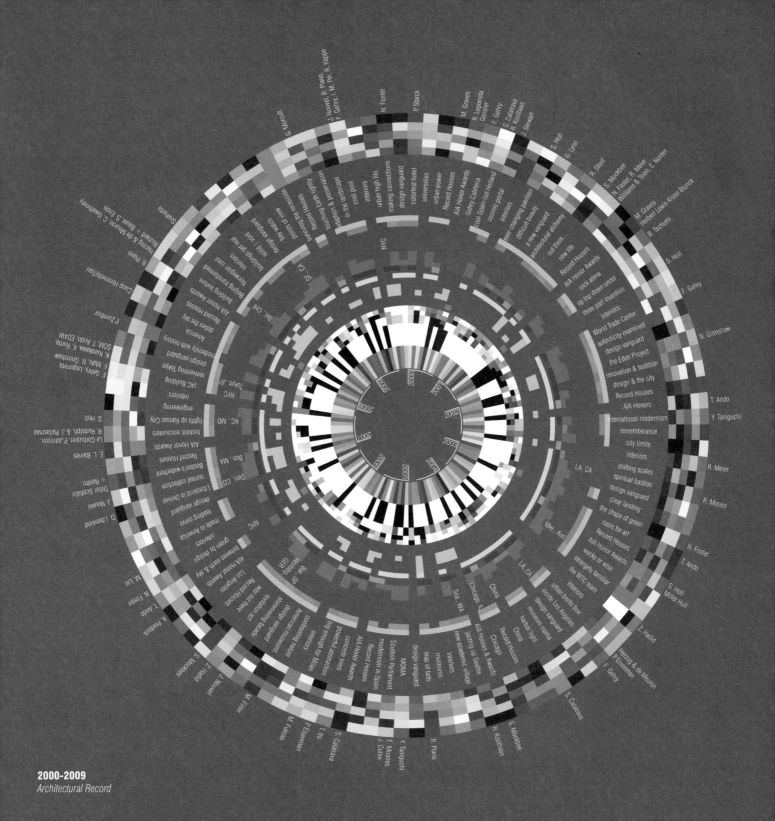

CHRYSLER BUILDING

VILLA SAVOYE

LE CENTRE GEORGES POMPIDOU

SYDNEY OPERA HOUSE

TJIBAOU CULTURAL CENTER

PEOPLE'S BUILDING

MAISON BORDEAUX

BORGES AND IRMAO BANK

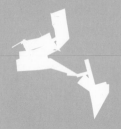

TVCC

PARTHENON

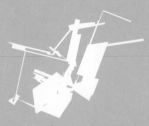

ALICE TULLY HALL

AUDITORIO KURSAAL

THORNCROWN CHAPEL

SEARS TOWER

INSTITUTE OF CONTEMPORARY ART

CASA DE CHÁ BOA NOVA

flattened façades

Architects love form. It was perhaps this love that compelled us to unroll these beautiful
buildings through a computer script in order to see what wonderful new forms emerged.

PORTUGUESE PAVILION

PORCHDOG HOUSE

PANTHEON

GUANGZHOU OPERA HOUSE

CCTV HEADQUARTERS

SPACE NEEDLE

BIRD'S NEST

BARCELONA PAVILION

BRASÍLIA CATHEDRAL

GUGGENHEIM, BILBAO

CASA DA MÚSICA

CATHEDRAL OF
OUR LADY OF THE ANGELS

ROBIE HOUSE

WENG CHAN TEMPLE

OSLO OPERA HOUSE

BANK OF CHINA TOWER

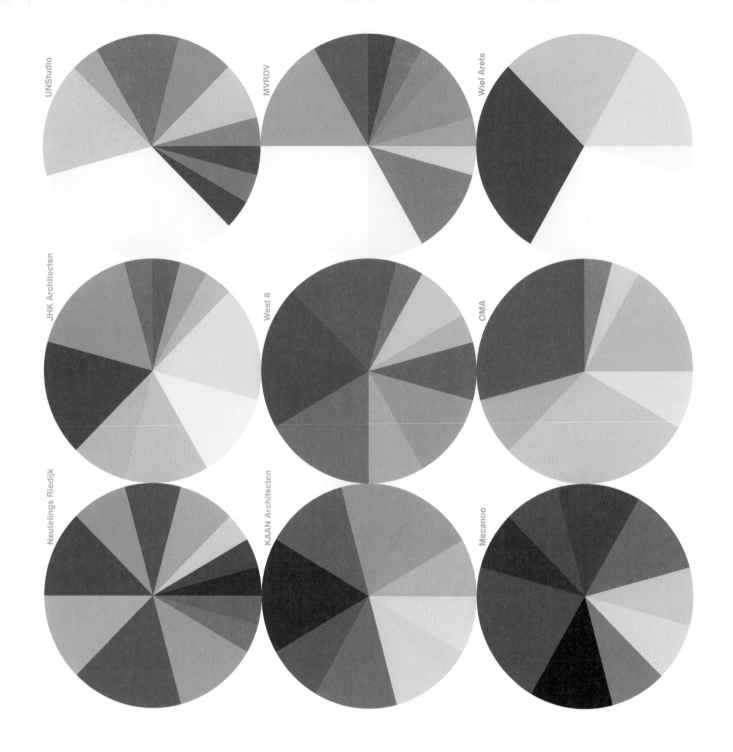

color pugilism: dutch vs. american

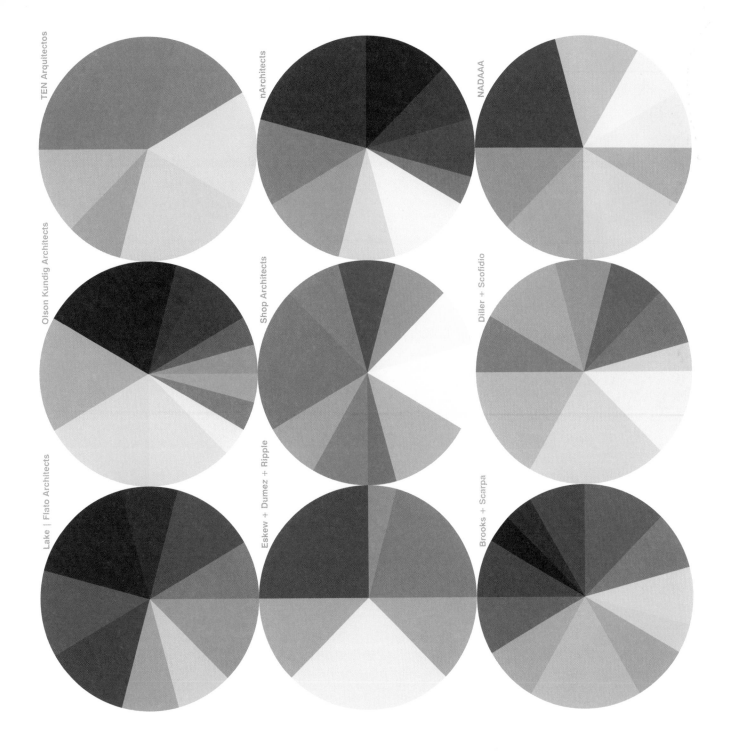

TEN Arquitectos

nArchitects

NADAAA

Olson Kundig Architects

Shop Architects

Diller + Scofidio

Lake | Flato Architects

Eskew + Dumez + Ripple

Brooks + Scarpa

What motivates architects to choose particular color palettes for their work? Can we recognize cultures through color in their respective built environments? This diagram maps some of the leading practitioners in Dutch and US architecture to compare the color choices in their work.

Caucasian 2009

ethnic minority 2009

ethnic minority 2005

homage to ethnic principals

Percentage of ethnic principals of American architecture firms.

ladies and gents

The ratio and evolution of licensed female to male practitioners in architecture since the AIA was founded in 1857.

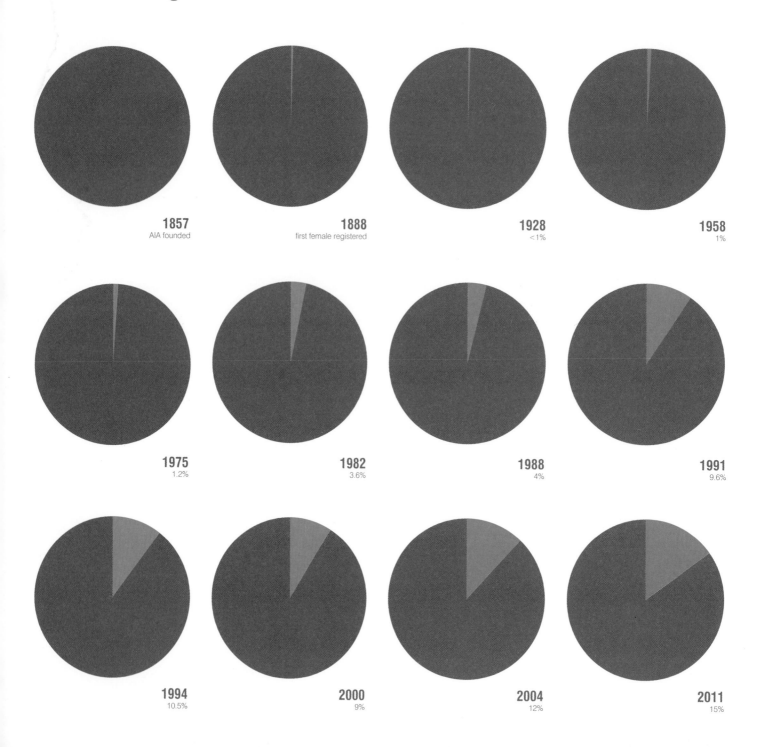

1857
AIA founded

1888
first female registered

1928
<1%

1958
1%

1975
1.2%

1982
3.6%

1988
4%

1991
9.6%

1994
10.5%

2000
9%

2004
12%

2011
15%

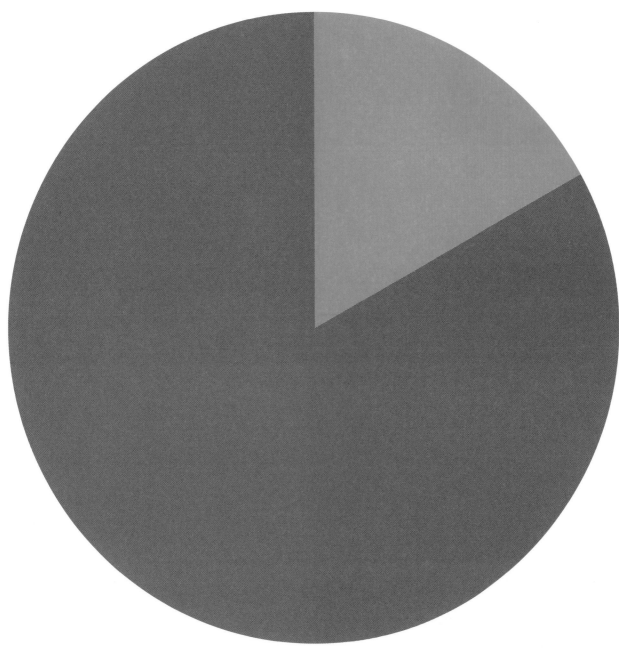

2013
17%

Wiel Arets Architects chromachrono

Wiel Arets (1986–present)
Selected works, 1986–2014.

Academy of Art & Architecture, 1993

Beligens Fashion Shop, 1986
De Waag Pharmacy, 1994
Police Station Vaals, 1995
KNSM Island Skydome, 1996

House & Studio Arets, 1997

AZL Pension Fund Headquarters, 1995

Police Station Boxtel, 1997
Lensvelt Factory & Office, 1999
Villa van Zanten, 2000

Hoge Heren, 2001

Hedge House, 2001
Kwakkel Showroom, 2002

Utrecht University Library, 2004

Music School, Heerlen, 2004

Glaspaleis, Heerlen, 2004
Sports Campus Leidsche Rijn, 2006

Euroborg Stadium, 2006

Hotel Zenden, 2009

Klooslertuin Housing, 2006
Gallery Borzo, 2006
Living Madrid, 2008
G' House, 2008
V' Tower, 2009

Four Towers Osdorp, 2010

De Nieuwe Liefde, 2011

H' House, 2011
Jellyfish House, 2013
B' Tower, 2013

E' Tower, 2013

A' House, 2014

AxB Tower, 2013
V' House, 2013
Schwäbisch Media, 22013
The Post, 2013

Allianz Headquarters, 2014

Truman Plaza, 2014
Regiocentrale Zuid, 2014

Campus Hoogvliet, 2014

IBA Housing, 1993

Vitra Fire Station, 1993
Landesgartenschau, 1999

Hoenheim-Nord Terminus Car Park, 2001

Bergisel Ski Jump, 2002
Lois & Richard Rosenthal Center for Contemporary Art, 2003
Ordrupgaard Museum Extension, 2005

BMW Central Building, 2005

Phaeno Science Centre, 2005

Maggie's Centre Fife, 2006
Burnham Pavilion, 2009

Spittelau Viaducts Housing Project, 2005
BMW Showroom, 2006
Nordpark Railway Stations, 2007

MAXXI: Museum of XXI Century Arts, 2009

JS Bach Chamber Music Hall, 2009

Mobile Art Chanel Contemporary Art Container, 2010

Guangzhou Opera House, 2010

Evelyn Grace Academy, 2010

Glasgow Riverside Museum of Transport, 2011
Roca London Gallery, 2011

London Aquatic Centre, 2011

Pierresvives, 2012

Eli & Edythe Broad Art Museum, 2012
Serpentine Sackler Gallery, 2013

Jockey Club Innovation Tower, 2014

Zaha Hadid Architects chromachrono

Zaha Hadid (1986–present)
Selected works, 1986–2014.

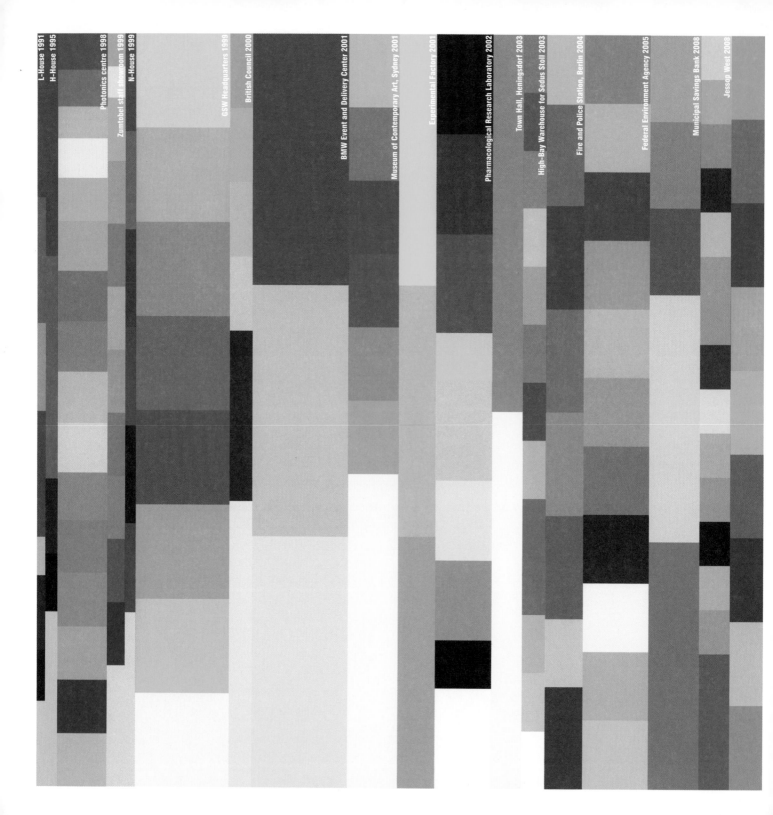

L-House 1991

H-House 1995

Photonics centre 1998

Zumtobel staff showroom 1999

N-House 1999

GSW Headquarters 1999

British Council 2000

BMW Event and Delivery Center 2001

Museum of Contemporary Art, Sydney 2001

Experimental Factory 2001

Pharmacological Research Laboratory 2002

Town Hall, Heningstorf 2003

High-Bay Warehouse for Sedus Stoll 2003

Fire and Police Station, Berlin 2004

Federal Environment Agency 2005

Municipal Savings Bank 2008

Jessop West 2008

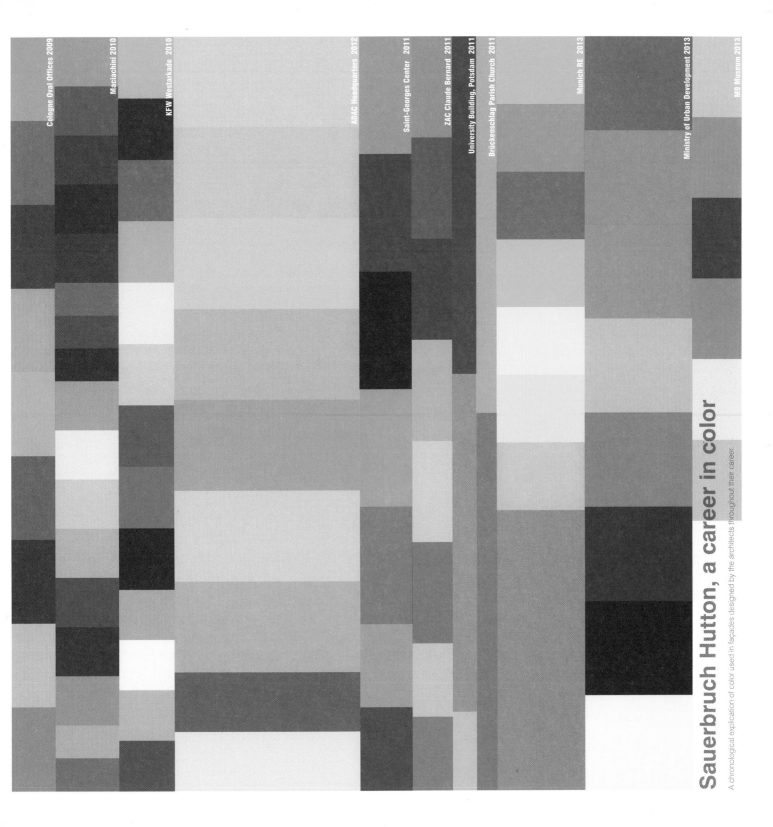

Cologne Oval Offices 2009

Maciachini 2010

KFW Westarkade 2010

ADAC Headquarters 2012

Saint-Georges Center 2011

ZAC Claude Bernard 2011

University Building, Potsdam 2011

Bruckenschlag Parish Church 2011

Munich RE 2013

Ministry of Urban Development 2013

M9 Museum 2013

Sauerbruch Hutton, a career in color

A chronological explication of color used in façades designed by the architects throughout their career.

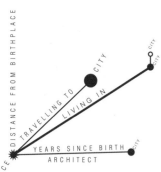

BIRTHPLACE • DISTANCE FROM BIRTHPLACE

TRAVELLING TO • CITY

LIVING IN • CITY

YEARS SINCE BIRTH • CITY

ARCHITECT

far from home

Architects are presented as constellations in this map that records their significant
geographic relocations and travels throughout their lifetimes.

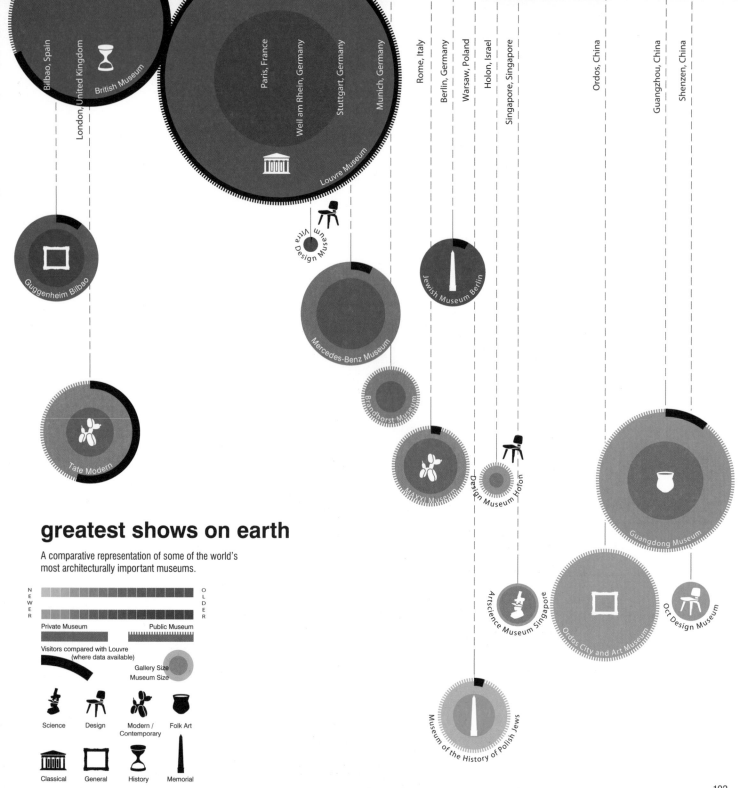

greatest shows on earth

A comparative representation of some of the world's most architecturally important museums.

NEWER — OLDER

Private Museum   Public Museum

Visitors compared with Louvre
(where data available)

Gallery Size
Museum Size

Science | Design | Modern / Contemporary | Folk Art

Classical | General | History | Memorial

Bilbao, Spain — British Museum
London, United Kingdom
Guggenheim Bilbao
Tate Modern

Paris, France — Louvre Museum
Weil am Rhein, Germany — Vitra Design Museum
Stuttgart, Germany — Mercedes-Benz Museum
Munich, Germany — Brandhorst Museum

Rome, Italy — MAXXI Museum
Berlin, Germany — Jewish Museum Berlin
Warsaw, Poland — Museum of the History of Polish Jews
Holon, Israel — Design Museum Holon
Singapore, Singapore — Artscience Museum Singapore

Ordos, China — Ordos City and Art Museum
Guangzhou, China — Guangdong Museum
Shenzen, China — Oct Design Museum

Pudong, China

Ningbo, China

Harbin, China

San Francisco, CA

Los Angeles, CA

Salt Lake City, UT

Denver, CO

Fort Worth, TX

Kansas City, MO

Bentonville, AR

New Orleans, LA

Atlanta, GA

East Lansing, MI

Ann Arbor, MI

Toronto, Canada

New York City, NY

Metropolitan Museum of Art

Solomon R. Guggenheim Museum

Whitney Museum

American Folk Art Museum

New Museum

Kimbell Art Museum

Kemper Museum

High Museum of Art

Getty Center

Ningbo Historic Museum

The Modern

The Gardiner Museum

de Young Museum

Denver Art Museum

Nelson-Atkins Museum of Art

University of Michigan Museum of Art

Los Angeles Museum of the Holocaust

Clyfford Still Museum

Crystal Bridges Museum

Eli & Edith Broad Museum

China Art Palace

China Wood Sculpture Museum

Natural History Museum of Utah

National World War II Museum

Whitney Museum (Piano Building) (1919)

Fumihiko Maki

Arata Isozaki

Kisho Kurokawa

Toyo Ito

QuaRtraits

Quick Response Codes were originally designed for the automotive industry in Japan. Though their normal use is as machine -readable codes that link to information in a separate location, they are also new visual forms that have embedded themselves in everyday contemporary life.

Each QR Code is a subtle yet unique visual form. In the spirit of the age and location in which they were born, and as a celebration of new visual readings, this diagram treats these codes as contemporary portraits of Japanese architectural practitioners.

Tadao Ando

Shigeru Ban

Kengo Kuma

Kazuyo Sejima

the painter's eye

Rembrandt

1 *Philosopher in Meditation* 1632
2 *Parable of the Labourers in the Vineyard* 1637
3 *The Night Watch* 1642
4 *Two Women and a Child* 1645
5 *The Holy Family* 1652

 1
 2
 3
 4
 5

Vermeer

1 *Officer and Laughing Girl* 1657
2 *The Music Lesson* 1662–1665
3 *The Art of Painting* 1666–1668
4 *Lady Standing at a Virginal* 1670–1672
5 *The Allegory of Faith* 1670–1672

 1
 2
 3
 4
 5

Matisse

1 *Red Room* 1908
2 *Red Studio* 1911
3 *Pink Studio* 1911
4 *Music Lesson* 1917
5 *Deux Fillettes, fond jaune et rouge* 1947

 1
 2
 3
 4
 5

Klee

1 *Blick auf eine Moschee* 1914
2 *Landscape and Yellow Church Tower* 1920
3 *Dream Studio* 1921
4 *Red Balloon* 1922
5 *Castle and Sun* 1928

 1
 2
 3
 4
 5

Braque

1 *Fauves* 1905
2 *The Church of Carrières-Saint-Denis* 1909
3 *Viaduct at L'Estaque* 1908
4 *Les Usines du Rio-Tinto à l'Estaque* 1910
5 *The Studio* 1910

 1
 2
 3
 4
 5

...a revelation of the colors that great painters used to convey architectural space.

Picasso

1
2
3
4

5

Van Gogh

1
2
3
4

5

Cézanne

1
2
3
4
5

Dalí

1
2
3
4
5

Kahlo

1
2
3
4
5

race to heaven

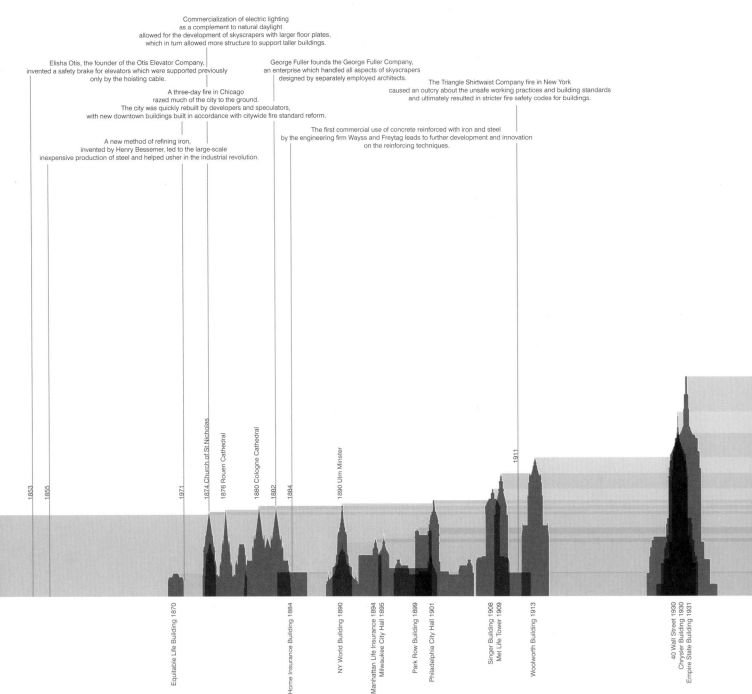

Commercialization of electric lighting
as a complement to natural daylight
allowed for the development of skyscrapers with larger floor plates,
which in turn allowed more structure to support taller buildings.

Elisha Otis, the founder of the Otis Elevator Company,
invented a safety brake for elevators which were supported previously
only by the hoisting cable.

George Fuller founds the George Fuller Company,
an enterprise which handled all aspects of skyscrapers
designed by separately employed architects.

The Triangle Shirtwaist Company fire in New York
caused an outcry about the unsafe working practices and building standards
and ultimately resulted in stricter fire safety codes for buildings.

A three-day fire in Chicago
razed much of the city to the ground.
The city was quickly rebuilt by developers and speculators,
with new downtown buildings built in accordance with citywide fire standard reform.

The first commercial use of concrete reinforced with iron and steel
by the engineering firm Wayss and Freytag leads to further development and innovation
on the reinforcing techniques.

A new method of refining iron,
invented by Henry Bessemer, led to the large-scale
inexpensive production of steel and helped usher in the industrial revolution.

1853
1855
1971
1874 Church of St.Nicholas
1876 Rouen Cathedral
1880 Cologne Cathedral
1882
1884
1890 Ulm Minster
1911

Equitable Life Building 1870
Home Insurance Building 1884
NY World Building 1890
Manhattan Life Insurance 1894
Milwaukee City Hall 1895
Park Row Building 1899
Philadelphia City Hall 1901
Singer Building 1908
Met Life Tower 1909
Woolworth Building 1913
40 Wall Street 1930
Chrysler Building 1930
Empire State Building 1931

Tracking the evolution of building height since the mid-nineteenth century.

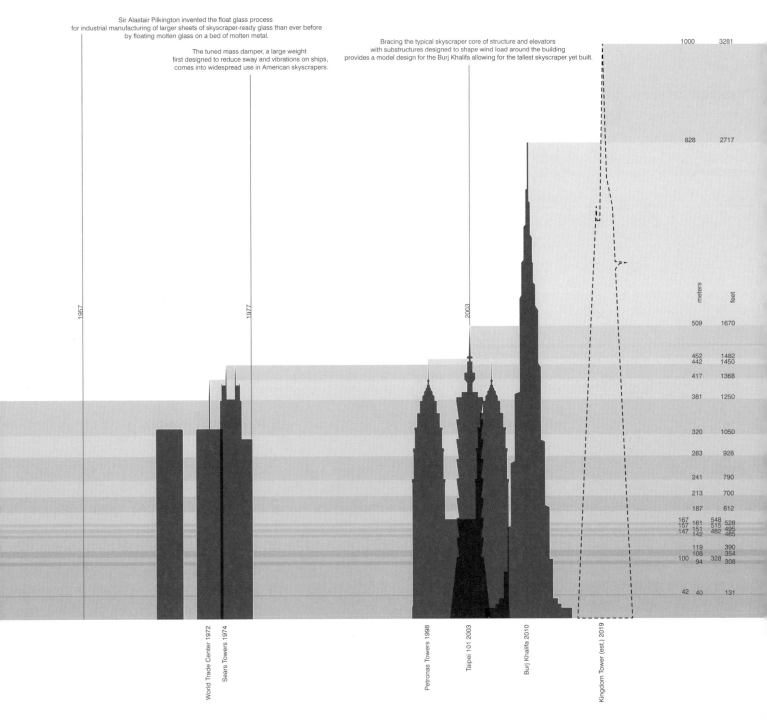

Sir Alastair Pilkington invented the float glass process
for industrial manufacturing of larger sheets of skyscraper-ready glass than ever before
by floating molten glass on a bed of molten metal.

The tuned mass damper, a large weight
first designed to reduce sway and vibrations on ships,
comes into widespread use in American skyscrapers.

Bracing the typical skyscraper core of structure and elevators
with substructures designed to shape wind load around the building
provides a model design for the Burj Khalifa allowing for the tallest skyscraper yet built.

1957

1977

2003

meters | feet

1000 | 3281

828 | 2717

509 | 1670

452 | 1482
442 | 1450

417 | 1368

381 | 1250

320 | 1050

283 | 928

241 | 790

213 | 700

187 | 612

167 | 161 | 548 | 528
157 | 151 | 515 | 495
147 | 142 | 482 | 465

119 | 390
108 | 354
100 | 94 | 328 | 308

42 | 40 | 131

World Trade Center 1972

Sears Towers 1974

Petronas Towers 1998

Taipei 101 2003

Burj Khalifa 2010

Kingdom Tower (est.) 2019

work
toward
mind thing
architectu
order
architect
construction like man spirit
day plan house
new
mass modern form lines great wall
light problem standard
life town
production art state Corbusier axis
room constructed elements same more
pure epoch tool engineer concrete window
regulation harmony revolution time
material human right airplanes
height large beautiful surface idea
street relationship Rome everything
arrangement old proportion machine limits city
another feet scale creation
building well little sense years
roof question Parthenon garden
geometry plastic decoration
place unity play interior whole
measure stone calculation simple
law rhythm principle perfection
factory mathematical towers
nature Michael Angelo
temple society villa practical
emotion Roman hand
view noble shade
enormous objects
front steel social
utilitarian industrial
family immense book logic
natural lumber present
labor reinforced Renaissance
painting outside water
effect universe automobile
Acropolis moment study
apses detail
drama rich single real
marble entrance primitive
furniture structure propylea
expression

C **K**

architecture
architect

building

city

form

house

man
woman

toward

towers

world

Le Corbusier

seminal koolcorb

Tracking word use in two seminal works of architecture,
Towards a New Architecture and *Delirious New York*.

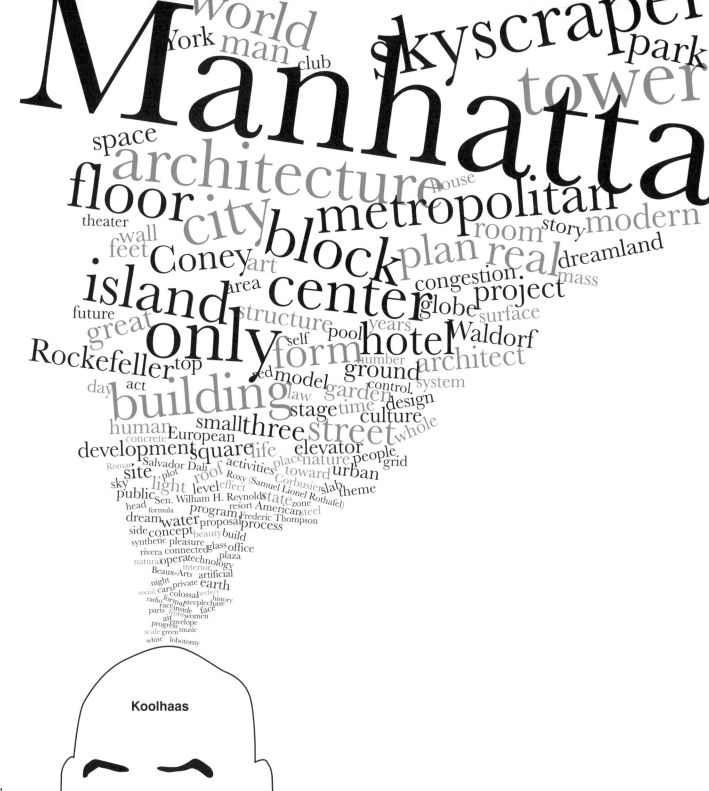

world skyscraper park
York man club tower

Manhatta

space house
architecture
floor city metropolitan room story modern
theater block plan real dreamland
wall feet Coney art congestion. project mass
island area center globe surface
future great structure years Waldorf
Rockefeller only self pool hotel architect
top red model ground number system
day act garden control.
building law stage time design culture
human small three street whole
development square life elevator people grid
concrete European activities nature urban
Roman Salvador Dali place toward slab
site plot Roxy (Samuel Lionel Rothafel) theme
sky light level roof Corbusier effect state zone
public Sen. Wilham H. Reynolds resort American steel
head formula program Frederic Thompson
dream water proposal process
side concept beauty build
synthetic pleasure glass office
rivera connected plaza
natural opera technology
Beaux-Arts interior artificial
night private earth
social cars colossal perfect
radio format steeplechase history
parts race inside face
front women
air envelope
progress
scale green music
white lobotomy

Koolhaas

111

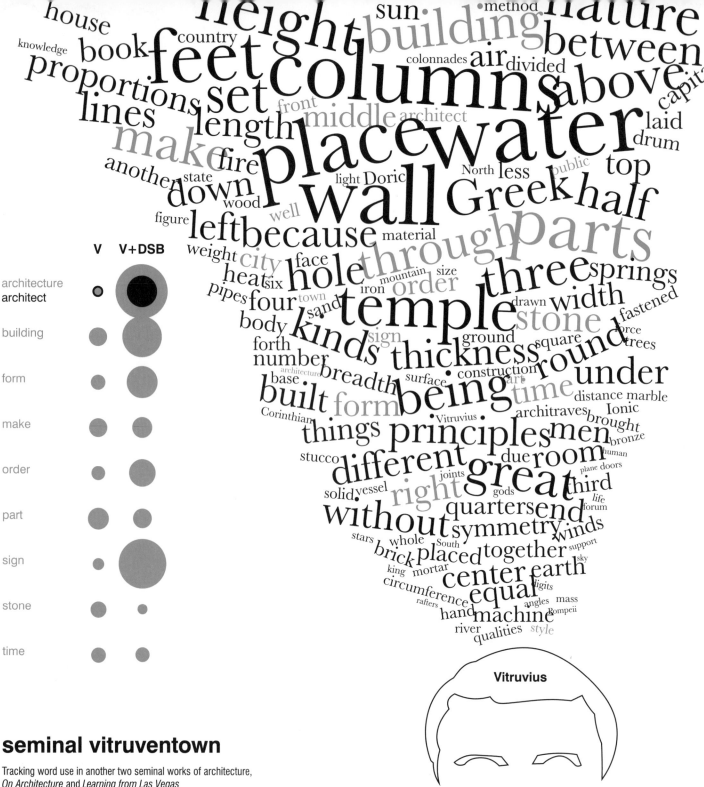

V V+DSB

architecture
architect
building
form
make
order
part
sign
stone
time

seminal vitruventown

Tracking word use in another two seminal works of architecture,
On Architecture and *Learning from Las Vegas*

Vitruvius

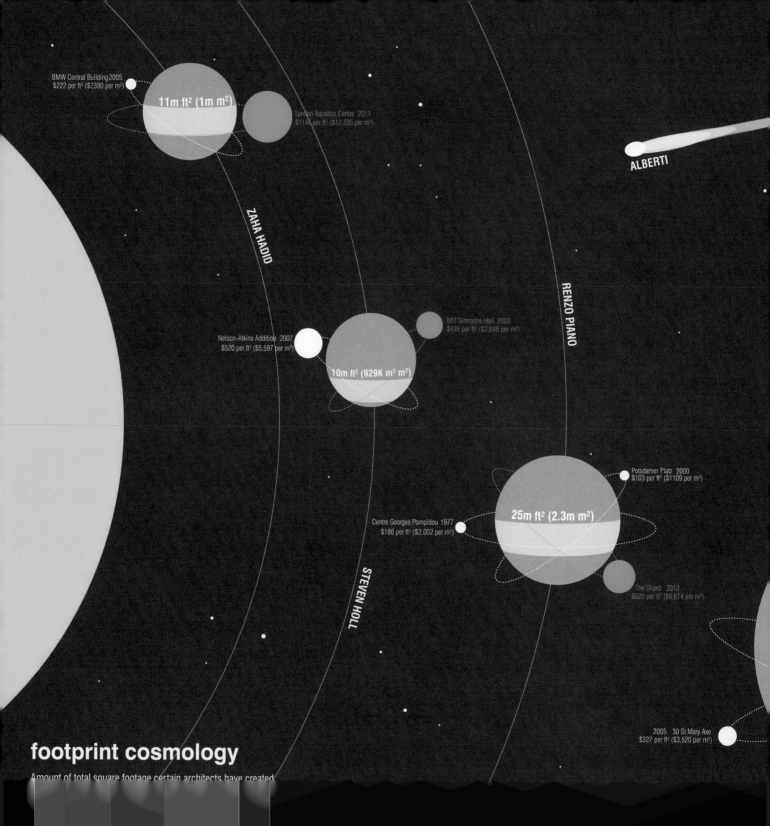

BMW Central Building 2005
$222 per ft² ($2390 per m²)

11m ft² (1m m²)

London Aquatics Centre 2011
$1145 per ft² ($12,335 per m²)

ALBERTI

ZAHA HADID

RENZO PIANO

MIT Simmons Hall 2002
$435 per ft² ($2,648 per m²)

Nelson-Atkins Addition 2007
$520 per ft² ($5,597 per m²)

10m ft² (929K m² m²)

Potsdamer Platz 2000
$103 per ft² ($1109 per m²)

Centre Georges Pompidou 1977
$186 per ft² ($2,002 per m²)

25m ft² (2.3m m²)

The Shard 2012
$620 per ft² ($6,674 per m²)

STEVEN HOLL

2005 30 St Mary Axe
$327 per ft² ($3,520 per m²)

footprint cosmology

Amount of total square footage certain architects have created

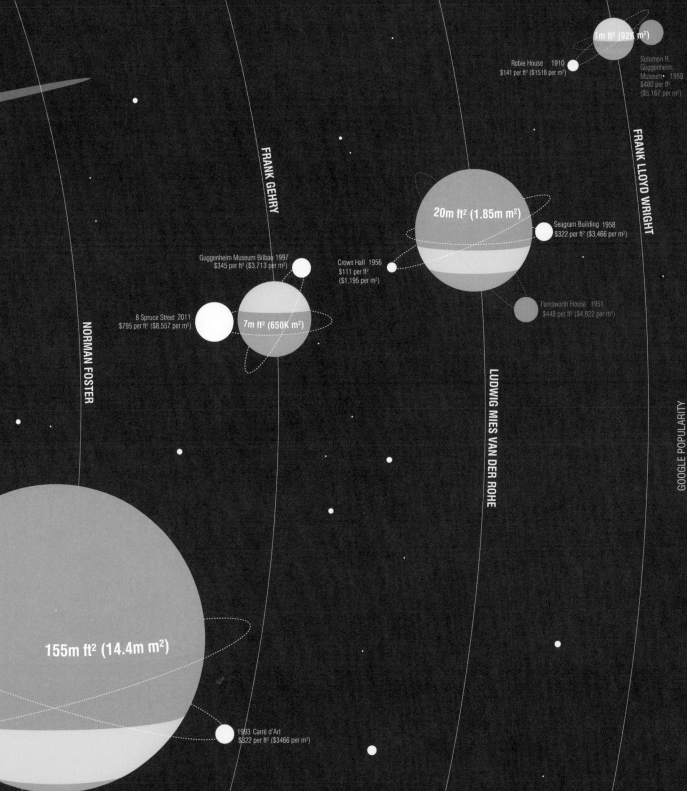

1m ft² (92K m²)

Robie House 1910
$141 per ft² ($1518 per m²)

Solomon R. Guggenheim Museum 1959
$480 per ft² ($5,167 per m²)

FRANK GEHRY

FRANK LLOYD WRIGHT

20m ft² (1.85m m²)

Seagram Building 1958
$322 per ft² ($3,466 per m²)

Guggenheim Museum Bilbao 1997
$345 per ft² ($3,713 per m²)

Crown Hall 1956
$111 per ft²
($1,195 per m²)

8 Spruce Street 2011
$795 per ft² ($8,557 per m²)

7m ft² (650K m²)

Farnsworth House 1951
$448 per ft² ($4,822 per m²)

NORMAN FOSTER

LUDWIG MIES VAN DER ROHE

155m ft² (14.4m m²)

1993 Carré d'Art
$322 per ft² ($3466 per m²)

GOOGLE POPULARITY

1,950,000
1,640,000
1,350,000
1,110,000
1,020,000
773,000
690,000

Size of satellites based on price per square foot

OVER BUDGET
UNDER BUDGET
RESIDENTIAL
INSTITUTIONAL
COMMERCIAL
URBAN

The Palazzo
HKS Inc.
Las Vegas

Wynn Resort
DeRuyter Butler
Glen Ashworth
Las Vegas

The Bellagio
DeRuyter Butler
Atlandia Design
Las Vegas

The Cosmopolitan
Friedmutter Group
& Arquitectonica
Las Vegas

One World Trade Center
David Childs
New York City

Yankee Stadium
Populous
New York

Wembley Stadium
Foster & Partners
London

tagged

Follow the QR Code links to discover the prices
of the most expensive buildings on the planet...

Princess Tower
Adnan Saffarini
Dubai

Antilla
Perkins + Will
Mumbai

Emirates Palace
John Elliott
Abu Dhabi

Marina Bay Sands
Moshe Safdie
Singapore

Resorts World Sentosa
Michael Graves
Singapore

Taipei 101
C Y Lee
& Partners
Taipei

Venetian Macau
Aedas
Macau

City of Dreams Casino
Arquitectonica
Macau

oh, what a tangled web we weave

Who individual architects cite as major influences on their careers.

Louis Kahn

Ludwig Mies van der Rohe

Rem Koolhaas

Kazimir Malevich

Erich
Mendelsohn

Alvar Aalto

Gian Lorenzo
Bernini

Francesco
Borromini

Jean Prouvé

Pier Luigi Nervi

Winy Maas

Zaha Hadid

Bjarke Ingels

Richard Meier

Renzo Piano

Moshe Safdie

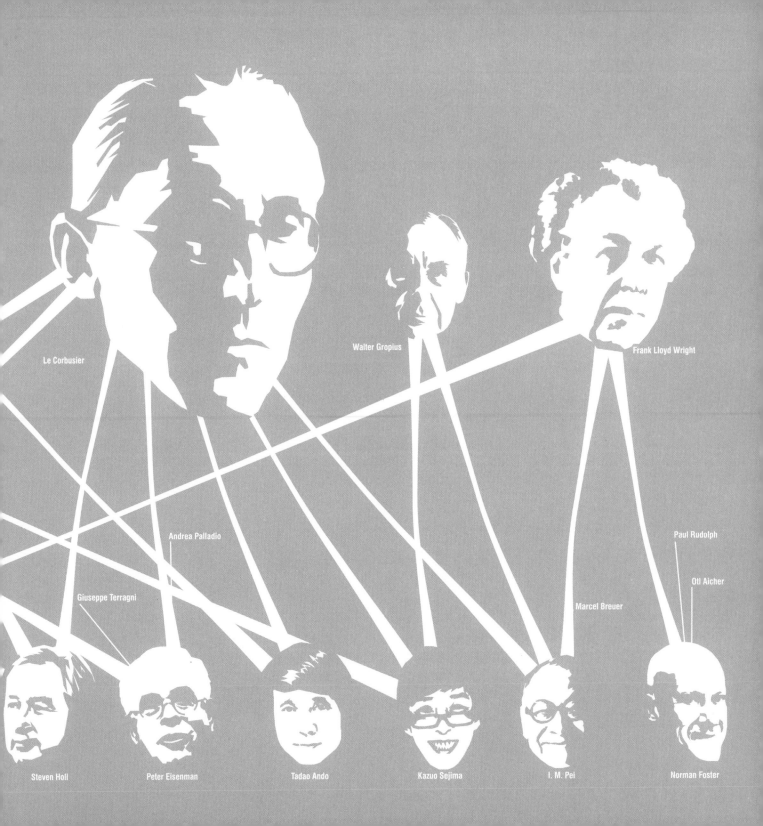

Le Corbusier

Walter Gropius

Frank Lloyd Wright

Andrea Palladio

Paul Rudolph

Otl Aicher

Giuseppe Terragni

Marcel Breuer

Steven Holl

Peter Eisenman

Tadao Ando

Kazuo Sejima

I. M. Pei

Norman Foster

the award goes to...

where do the winners of architecture's
most prestigious awards reside?

● Royal Gold Medal
● AIA Gold Medal
● AIA Architecture Firm Awards
● Thomas Jefferson Medal in Architecture
● Alvar Aalto Medal
● Pritzker Prize
● Wolf Prize in the Arts
● UIA Gold Medal
● Erich Schelling Architecture Award
● Jane Drew Prize

this will kill that

urban ecliptic Relating population, area, and age in the world's major urban centers.

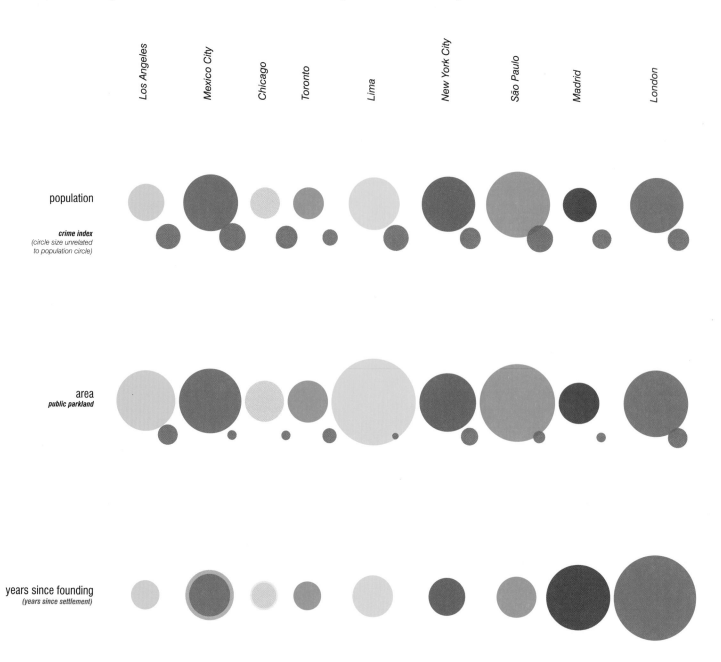

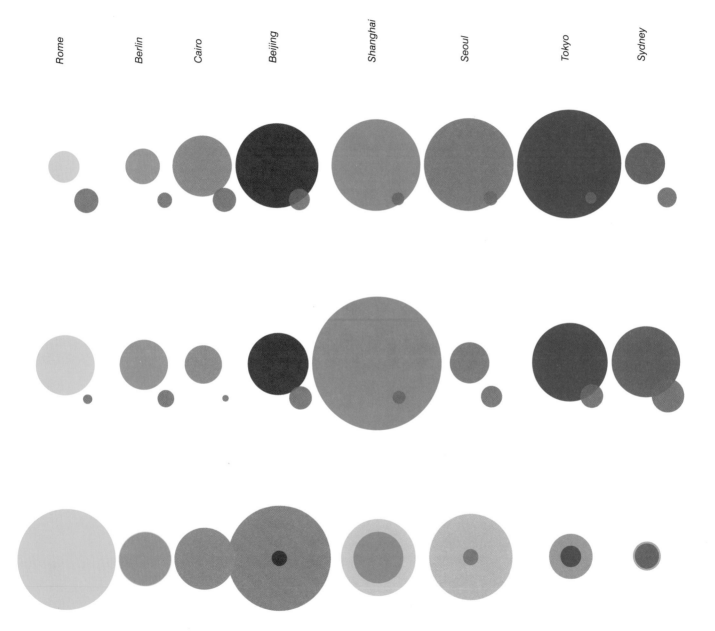

Rome Berlin Cairo Beijing Shanghai Seoul Tokyo Sydney

as the crow flies

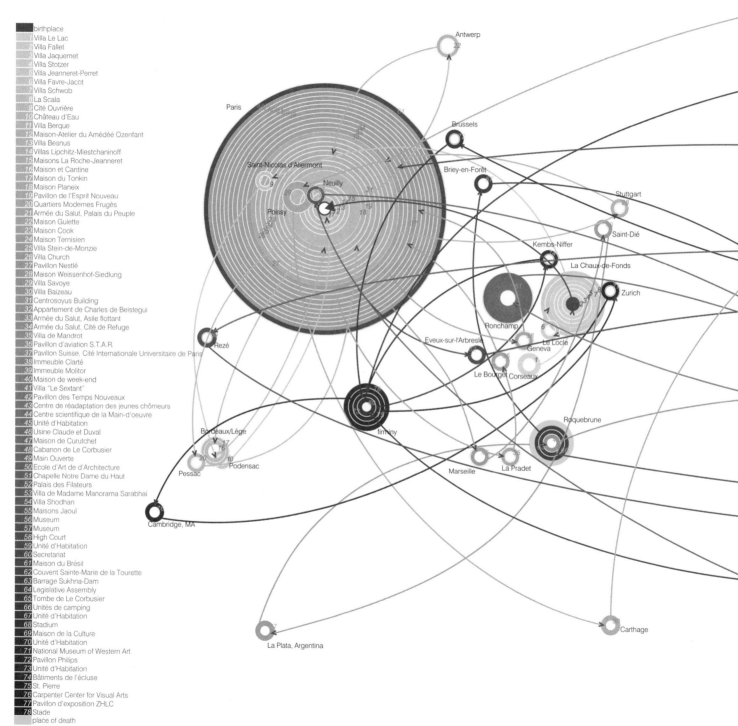

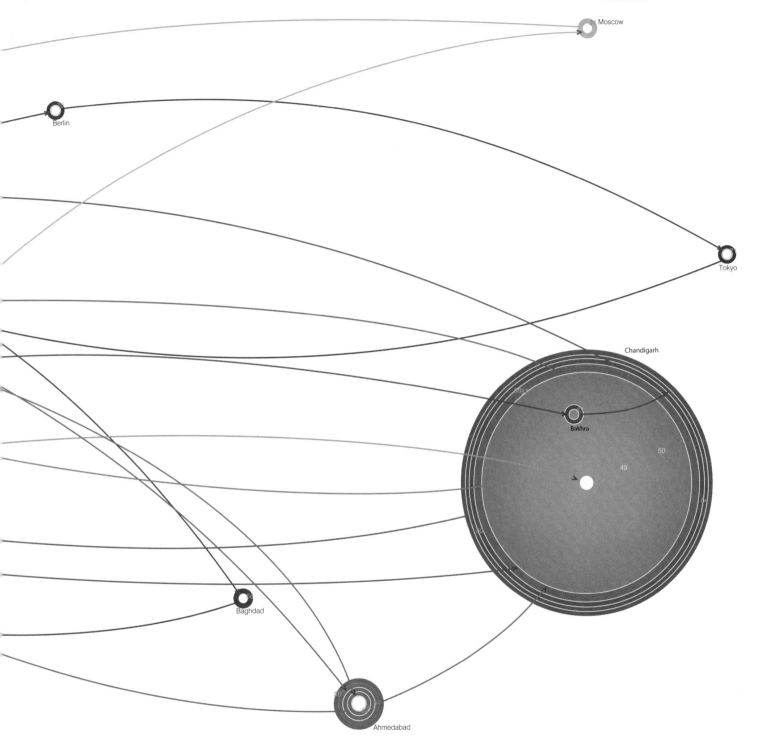

Moscow

Berlin

Tokyo

Chandigarh

Bakhra

50

49

Baghdad

Ahmedabad

*A migration diagram of Le Corbusier ("The Crow") and
his 78 buildings in chronological order by shade.*

white out

A comprehensive diagram of color in the work of Richard Meier.

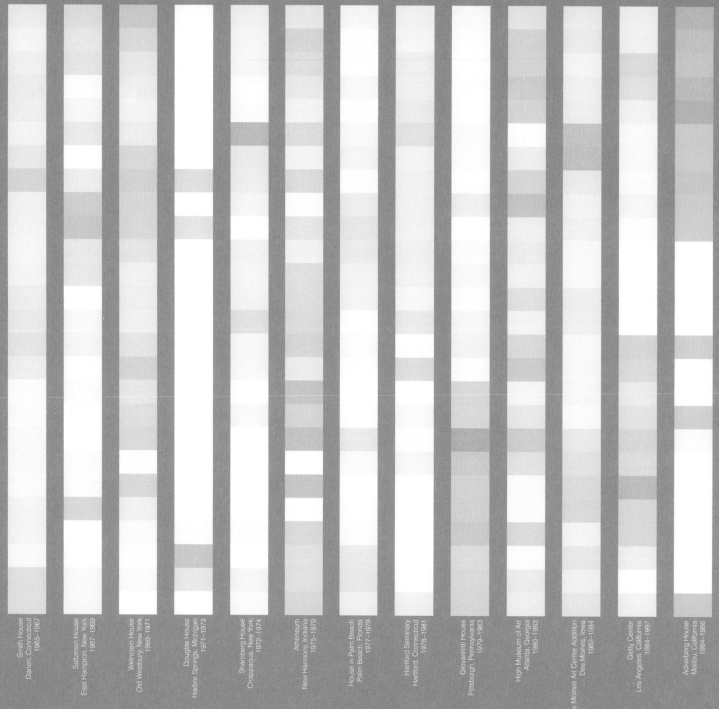

Smith House
Darien, Connecticut
1965–1967

Saltzman House
East Hampton, New York
1967–1969

Weinstein House
Old Westbury, New York
1969–1971

Douglas House
Harbor Springs, Michigan
1971–1973

Shamberg House
Chappaqua, New York
1972–1974

Atheneum
New Harmony, Indiana
1975–1979

House in Palm Beach
Palm Beach, Florida
1977–1979

Hartford Seminary
Hartford, Connecticut
1978–1981

Giovannitti House
Pittsburgh, Pennsylvania
1979–1983

High Museum of Art
Atlanta, Georgia
1980–1983

Des Moines Art Center Addition
Des Moines, Iowa
1982–1984

Getty Center
Los Angeles, California
1984–1997

Ackerberg House
Malibu, California
1984–1986

wait, white ain't white?

Shades of white reflected off the surfaces of Richard Meier's work from 1965–2011.

130

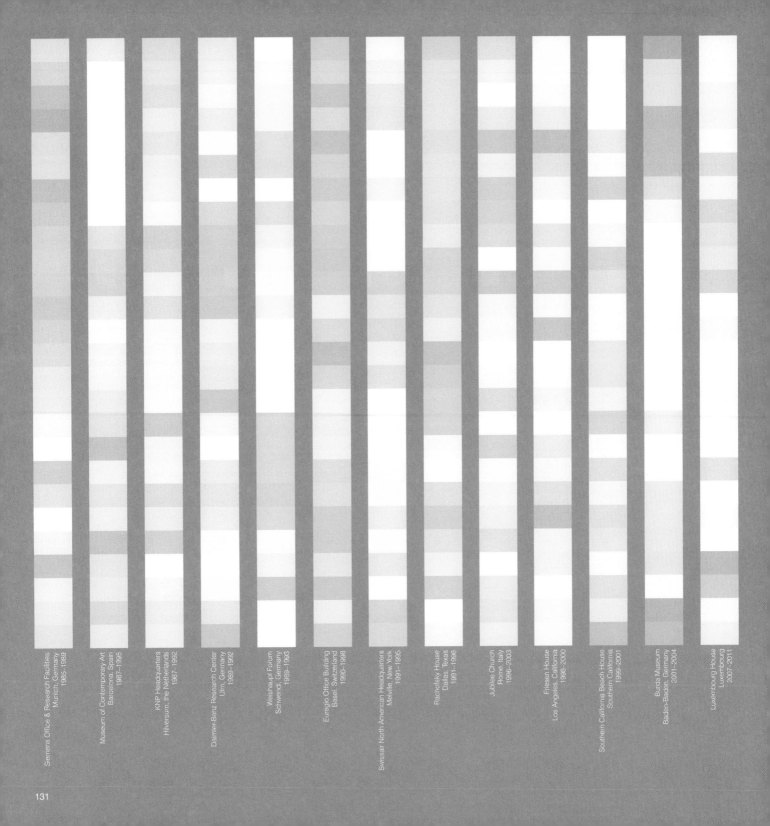

Siemens Office & Research Facilities
Munich, Germany
1985–1989

Museum of Contemporary Art
Barcelona, Spain
1987–1995

KNP Headquarters
Hilversum, the Netherlands
1987–1992

Daimler-Benz Research Center
Ulm, Germany
1989–1992

Weishaupt Forum
Schwendi, Germany
1989–1993

Euregio Office Building
Basel, Switzerland
1990–1998

Swissair North American Headquarters
Melville, New York
1991–1995

Racholfsky House
Dallas, Texas
1991–1996

Jubilee Church
Rome, Italy
1996–2003

Friesen House
Los Angeles, California
1998–2000

Southern California Beach House
Southern California
1999–2001

Burda Museum
Baden-Baden, Germany
2001–2004

Luxembourg House
Luxembourg
2007–2011

Absolute World Towers

House of the Arts

The Sha

Casa da I

Perot Museum of Natural Sciences

Seattle Public Library

Disney Concert Hall

30 St Mary Ax

Eden Pro

Basket Building

CN Tower

John Hancock Center

Sears Tower

Torre Galatea   Lloyd's Building

Cathedral of Brasília

Habitat 67

Montreal Biosphere

Space Needle

S

Guggenheim Muse

Chrysler Building

Casa Milà   Ideal Palace

La Sagrada Fa

Big Ben

Arc de Triomphe

New Palace Potsdam

Notre-Dame

C

bucket list

A wordcloud generated by a general internet search for the most popular buildings to visit before you die.

...uel Station+ McDonald's

Gardens by the Bay

Sutyagin House

Grand Lisboa

National Library of Belarus

Zénith de Strasbourg

...sica

Taipei 101

Petronas Towers

Krzywy Domek

Burj Khalifa

Forest Spiral

...t

One Canada Square

Dancing Building

Lotus Temple India

Cube Houses

...ney Opera House

...m

Atomium

...ília

...ng Tower of Pisa

Taj Mahal

...osseum

Hagia Sophia

Great Wall of China

Pantheon

The Ten Books on Architecture

The Four Books on Architecture

An Essay on Architecture

The Seven Lamps of Architecture

The Poetry of Architecture

Architecture

Towards a New Architecture

Complexity and Contradiction in Architecture

The Architecture of the City

Programs and Manifestos on 20th-century Architecture

Delirious New York

Modern Architecture Since 1900

Vitruvius

Palladio

Laugier

Ruskin

Ruskin

Meugens Bell

Le Corbusier

Venturi

Rossi

Conrads

Koolhaas

Curtis

Book Length

Popularity (Amazon Architecture Rank) →

History
Reference
Specialty
Introductory
Theory

hot canon, not canon

Which architecture texts are REALLY hot, and which are not?

Architecture Theory
Since 1968

Hays

Architecture:
Form, Space, and Order

Ching

101 Things I Learned in Architecture School

Frederick

Architecture: A World Histroy

Borden, Elzanowski,
Taylor, Tuerk

The Architecture of Happiness

de Botton

A Visual Dictionary of Architecture

Ching

The Architecture Reference
+ Specification Book

Wheeler,
McMorrough

Architecture in Photographs

Baldwin

Archidoodle: the Architect's Activity Book

Bowkett

Lego Architecture:
the Visual Guide

Dillon,
Biesty,
Wilkinson

The Story of Buildings

architectural eras

A comparison of the characteristics of significant periods in architectural history.

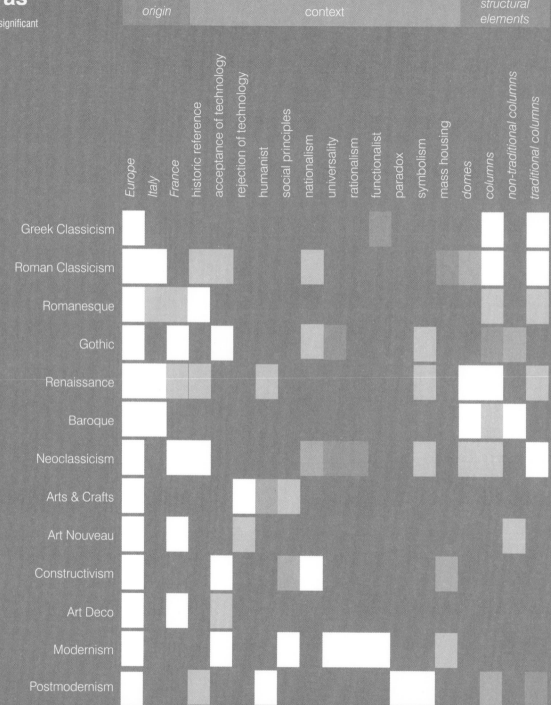

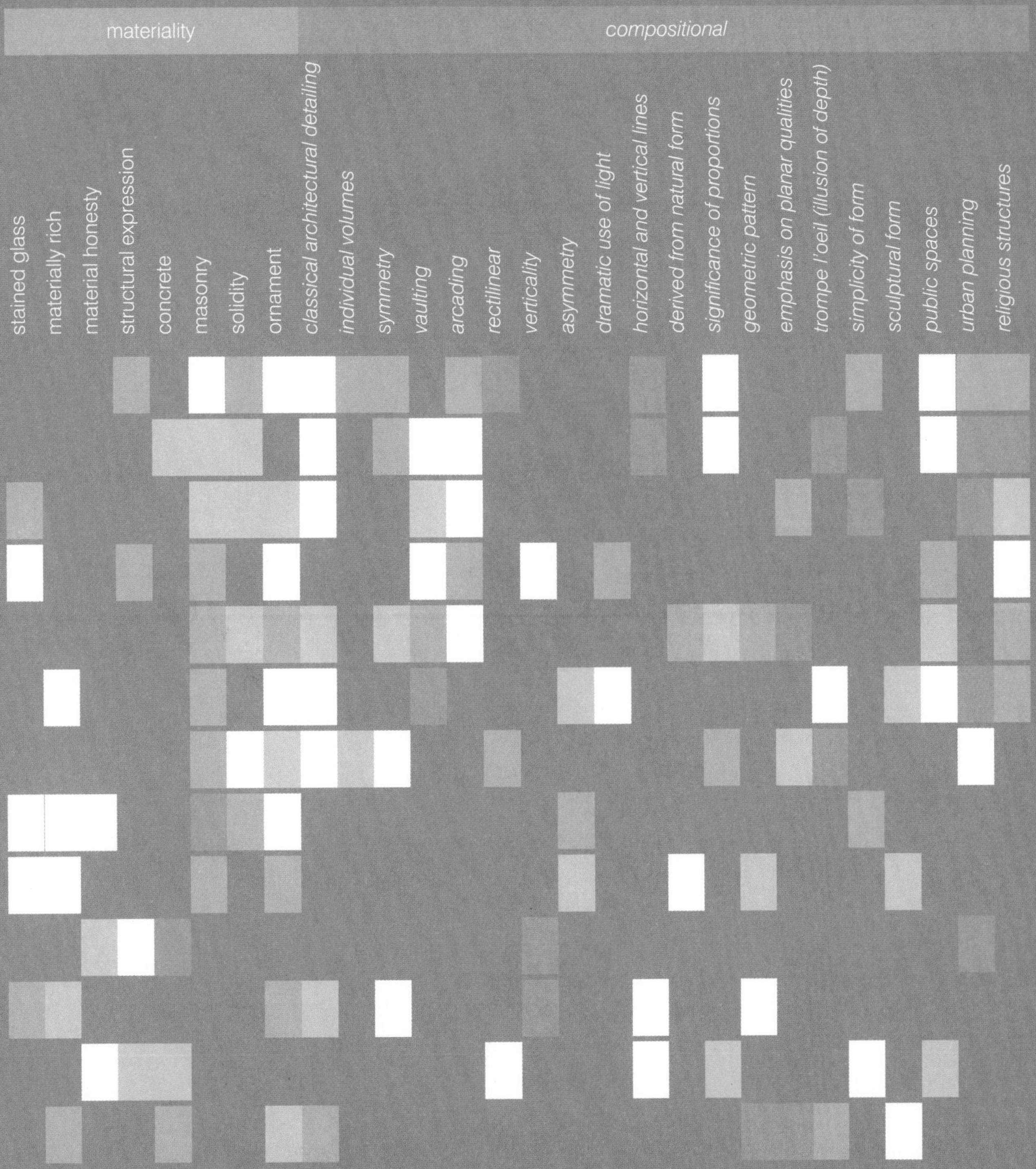

materiality
compositional
stained glass
materially rich
material honesty
structural expression
concrete
masonry
solidity
ornament
classical architectural detailing
individual volumes
symmetry
vaulting
arcading
rectilinear
verticality
asymmetry
dramatic use of light
horizontal and vertical lines
derived from natural form
significance of proportions
geometric pattern
emphasis on planar qualities
trompe l'oeil (illusion of depth)
simplicity of form
sculptural form
public spaces
urban planning
religious structures

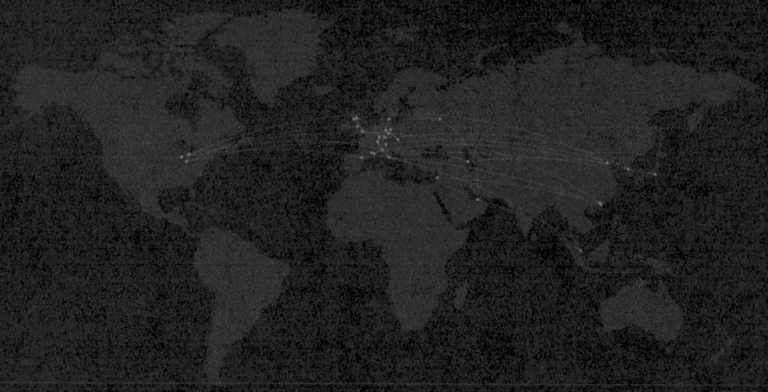

Zaha Hadid

Steven Holl

Tod Williams Billie Tsien

Sobejano Arquitectos

flight paths (individual)

OMA

Herzog & de Meuron

Frank Gehry

UNStudio

Mapping individual architects' project locations in a globalized world.

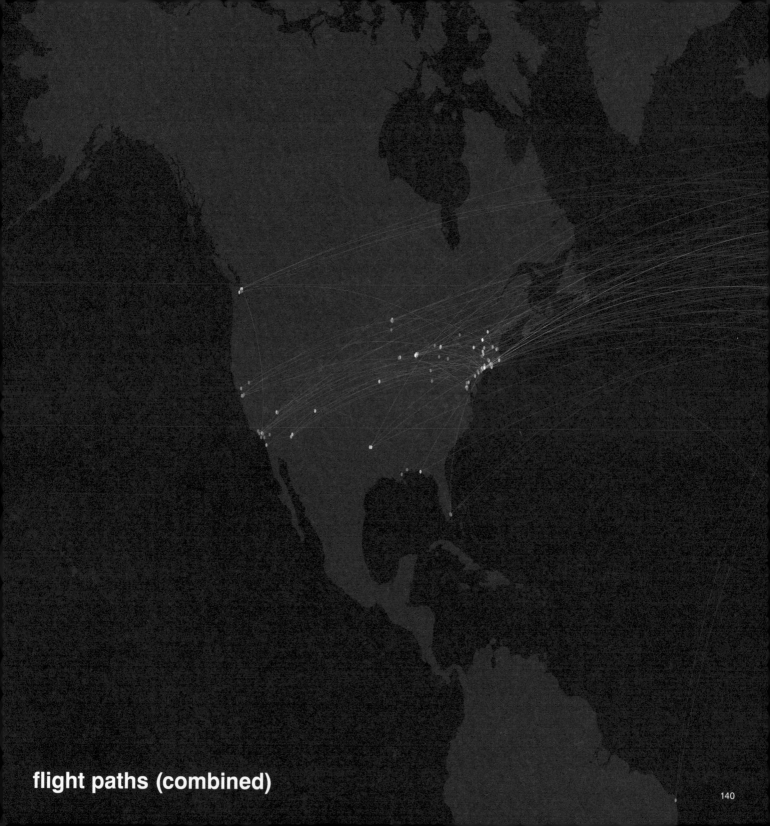

flight paths (combined)

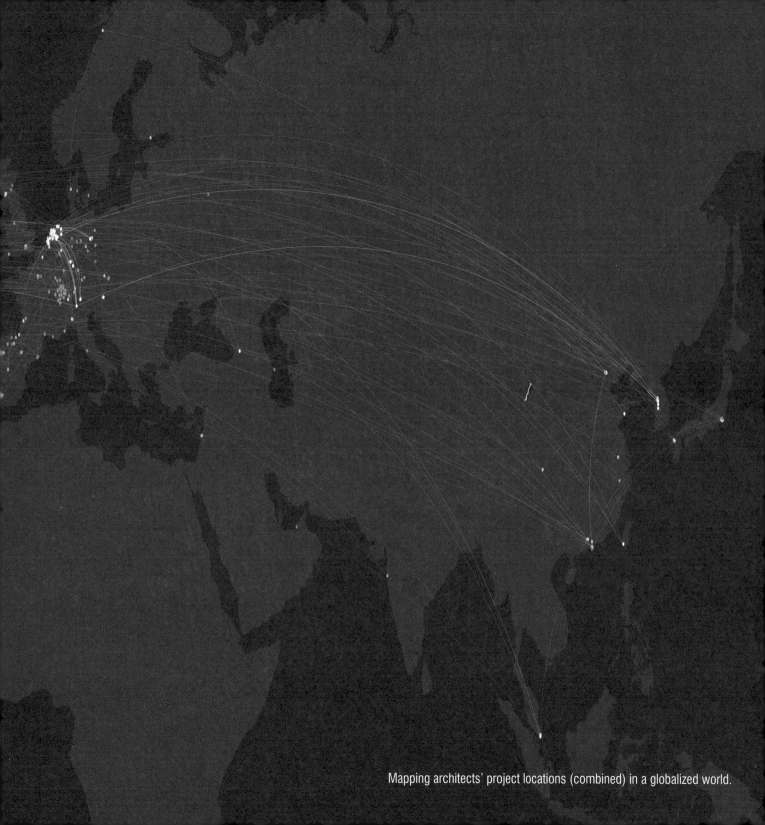

Mapping architects' project locations (combined) in a globalized world.

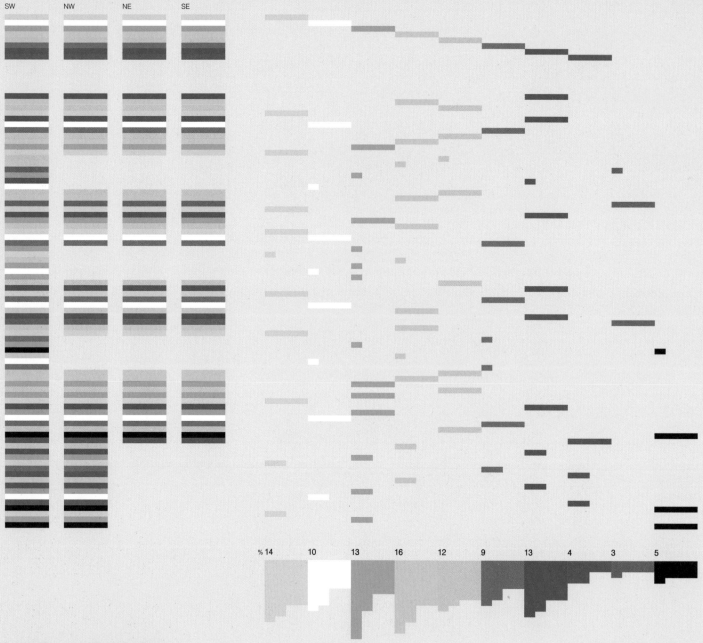

berlin ex[skin]d

A deconstruction of the colorful envelopes of Petersen Architeckten's Berlin Airport Hotel and Sauerbruch Hutton's Fire & Police Station, parsing colors into their occurrence on particular building faces, and quantifying the colors into their respective percentages.

Berlin Airport Hotel
Petersen Architeckten
2012
Berlin, DE

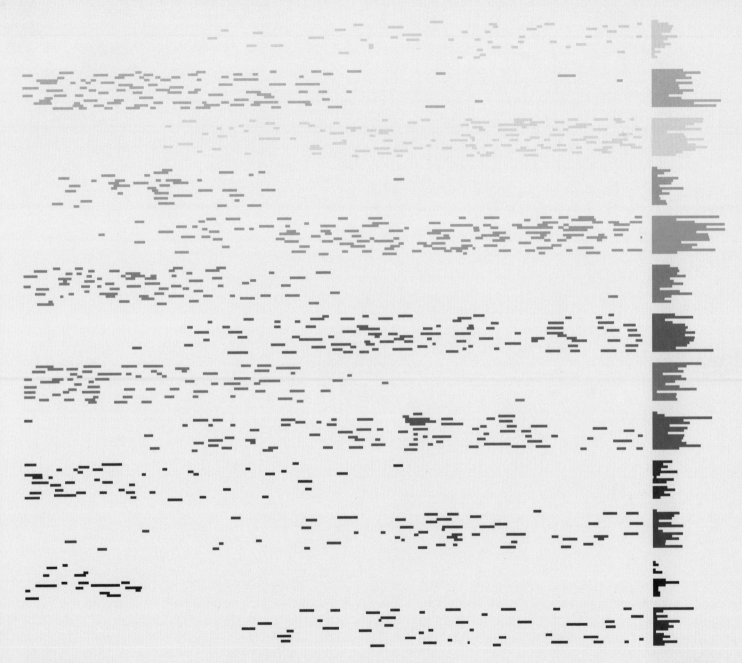

Fire & Police Station
Sauerbruch Hutton
2004
Berlin, DE

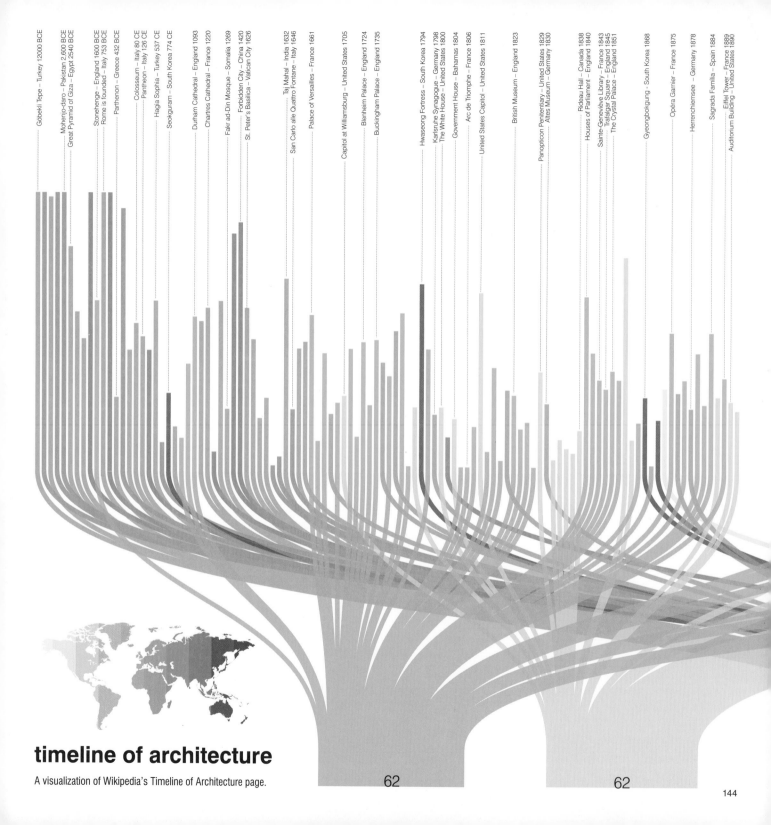

Göbekli Tepe – Turkey 12000 BCE
Mohenjo-daro – Pakistan 2,600 BCE
Great Pyramid of Giza – Egypt 2540 BCE
Stonehenge – England 1600 BCE
Rome is founded – Italy 753 BCE
Parthenon – Greece 432 BCE
Colosseum – Italy 80 CE
Pantheon – Italy 126 CE
Hagia Sophia – Turkey 537 CE
Seokguram – South Korea 774 CE
Durham Cathedral – England 1093
Chartres Cathedral – France 1220
Fakr ad-Din Mosque – Somalia 1269
Forbidden City – China 1420
St. Peter's Basilica – Vatican City 1626
Taj Mahal – India 1632
San Carlo alle Quattro Fontane – Italy 1646
Palace of Versailles – France 1661
Capitol at Williamsburg – United States 1705
Blenheim Palace – England 1724
Buckingham Palace – England 1735
Hwaseong Fortress – South Korea 1794
Karlsruhe Synagogue – Germany 1798
The White House – United States 1800
Government House – Bahamas 1804
Arc de Triomphe – France 1806
United States Capitol – United States 1811
British Museum – England 1823
Panopticon Penitentiary – United States 1829
Altes Museum – Germany 1830
Rideau Hall – Canada 1838
Houses of Parliament – England 1840
Sainte-Geneviève Library – France 1843
Trafalgar Square – England 1845
The Crystal Palace – England 1851
Gyeongbokgung – South Korea 1868
Opéra Garnier – France 1875
Herrenchiemsee – Germany 1878
Sagrada Família – Spain 1884
Eiffel Tower – France 1889
Auditorium Building – United States 1890

timeline of architecture

A visualization of Wikipedia's Timeline of Architecture page.

62

62

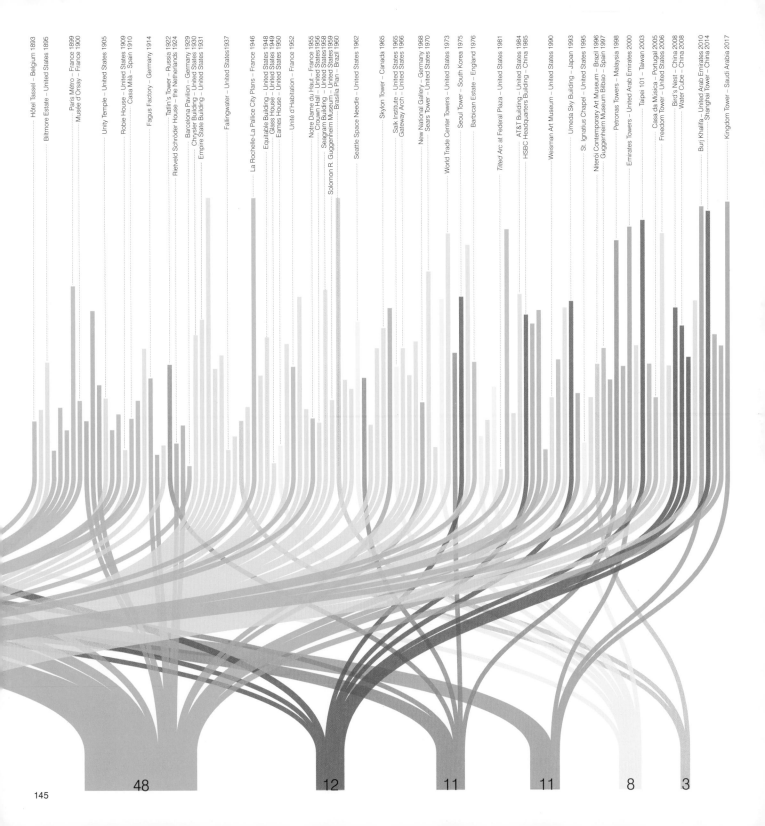

Hôtel Tassel – Belgium 1893
Biltmore Estate – United States 1895
Paris Métro – France 1899
Musée d'Orsay – France 1900
Unity Temple – United States 1905
Robie House – United States 1909
Casa Milà – Spain 1910
Fagus Factory – Germany 1914
Tatlin's Tower – Russia 1922
Rietveld Schröder House – the Netherlands 1924
Barcelona Pavilion – Germany 1929
Chrysler Building – United States 1930
Empire State Building – United States 1931
Fallingwater – United States 1937
La Rochelle-La Pallice City Plans – France 1946
Equitable Building – United States 1948
Glass House – United States 1949
Eames House – United States 1950
Unité d'Habitation – France 1952
Notre Dame du Haut – France 1955
Crown Hall – United States 1956
Seagram Building – United States 1958
Solomon R. Guggenheim Museum – United States 1959
Brasília Plan – Brazil 1960
Seattle Space Needle – United States 1962
Skylon Tower – Canada 1965
Salk Institute – United States 1965
Gateway Arch – United States 1966
New National Gallery – Germany 1968
Sears Tower – United States 1970
World Trade Center Towers – United States 1973
Seoul Tower – South Korea 1975
Barbican Estate – England 1976
Tilted Arc at Federal Plaza – United States 1981
AT&T Building – United States 1984
HSBC Headquarters Building – China 1985
Weisman Art Museum – United States 1990
Umeda Sky Building – Japan 1993
St. Ignatius Chapel – United States 1995
Niterói Contemporary Art Museum – Brazil 1996
Guggenheim Museum Bilbao – Spain 1997
Petronas Towers – Malaysia 1998
Emirates Towers – United Arab Emirates 2000
Casa da Música – Portugal 2005
Freedom Tower – United States 2006
Bird's Nest – China 2008
Water Cube – China 2008
Burj Khalifa – United Arab Emirates 2010
Shanghai Tower – China 2014
Kingdom Tower – Saudi Arabia 2017

48   12   11   11   8   3

145

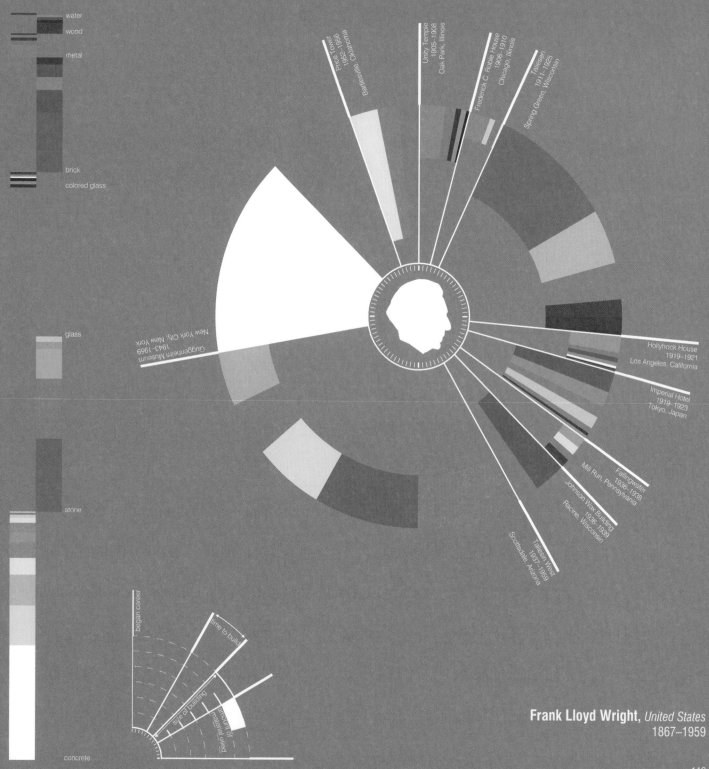

water
wood
metal
brick
colored glass

glass

stone

concrete

began career
time to build
size of building
amount of material used

Price Tower
1952–1956
Bartlesville, Oklahoma

Unity Temple
1905–1908
Oak Park, Illinois

Frederick C. Robie House
1908–1910
Chicago, Illinois

Taliesen
1911–1925
Spring Green, Wisconsin

Guggenheim Museum
1943–1959
New York City, New York

Hollyhock House
1919–1921
Los Angeles, California

Imperial Hotel
1919–1923
Tokyo, Japan

Fallingwater
1936–1938
Mill Run, Pennsylvania

Johnson Wax Building
1936–1939
Racine, Wisconsin

Taliesin West
1937–1959
Scottsdale, Arizona

Frank Lloyd Wright, *United States*
1867–1959

146

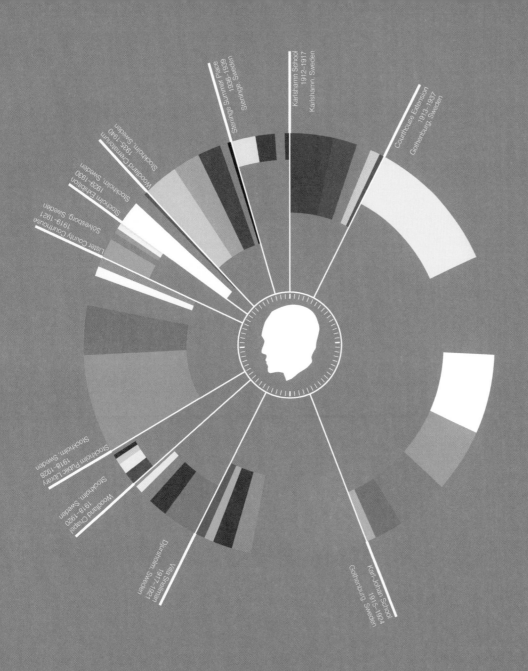

Karlshamn School
1912–1917
Karlshamn, Sweden

Steninge Summer Place
1936–1939
Steninge, Sweden

Courthouse Extension
1913–1937
Gothenburg, Sweden

Woodland Crematorium
1935–1940
Stockholm, Sweden

Stockholm Exhibition
1929–1930
Stockholm, Sweden

Lister County Courthouse
1919–1921
Solvesborg, Sweden

Stockholm Public Library
1918–1928
Stockholm, Sweden

Woodland Chapel
1918–1920
Stockholm, Sweden

Villa Snellman
1917–1921
Djursholm, Sweden

Karl-Johan School
1915–1924
Gothenburg, Sweden

tile

concrete

wood

metal

brick

stone

glass

stucco

Erik Gunnar Asplund, *Sweden*
1885–1940

147

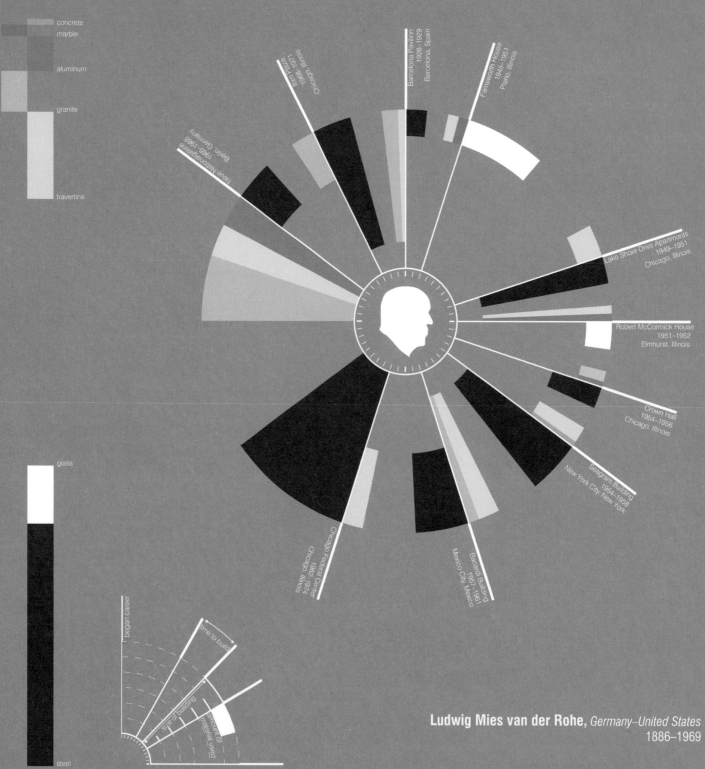

concrete
marble
aluminum
granite
travertine

glass
steel

Barcelona Pavilion
1928–1929
Barcelona, Spain

Farnsworth House
1945–1951
Plano, Illinois

IBM Plaza
1968–1971
Chicago, Illinois

Neue Nationalgalerie
1965–1968
Berlin, Germany

Lake Shore Drive Apartments
1949–1951
Chicago, Illinois

Robert McCormick House
1951–1952
Elmhurst, Illinois

Crown Hall
1954–1956
Chicago, Illinois

Seagram Building
1954–1958
New York City, New York

Bacardi Building
1957–1961
Mexico City, Mexico

Chicago Federal Center
1962–1974
Chicago, Illinois

began career

time to build

size of building

amount of
material used

Ludwig Mies van der Rohe, *Germany–United States*
1886–1969

148

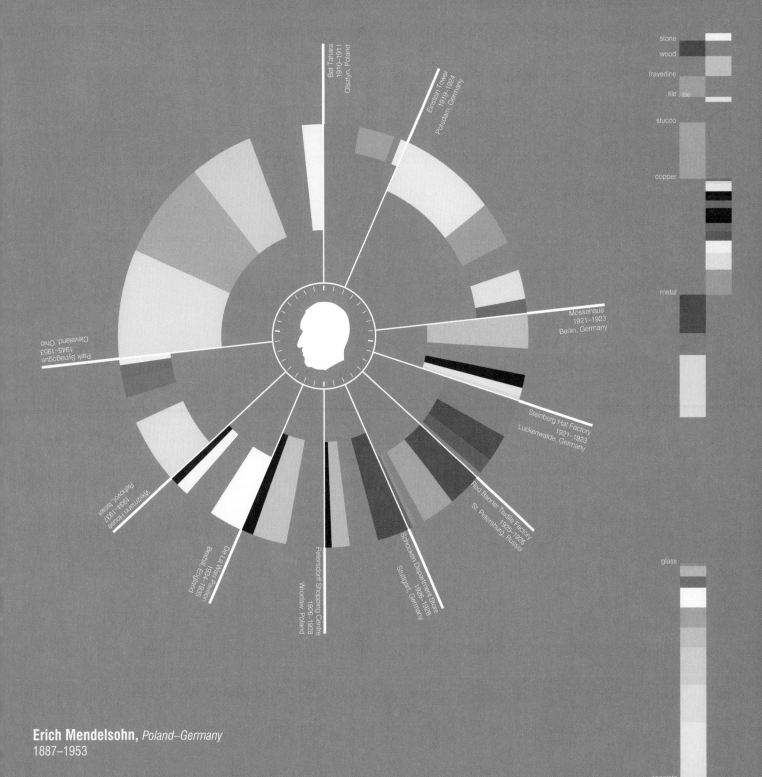

stone
wood
travertine
tile · tile
stucco
copper
metal
glass
concrete

Bel Tahara
1910–1911
Olsztyn, Poland

Einstein Tower
1919–1924
Potsdam, Germany

Mossehaus
1921–1923
Berlin, Germany

Steinberg Hat Factory
1921–1923
Luckenwalde, Germany

Red Banner Textile Factory
1925–1926
St. Petersburg, Russia

Schocken Department Store
1926–1928
Stuttgart, Germany

Petersdorff Shopping Centre
1926–1928
Wrocław, Poland

De La Warr Pavilion
1934–1935
Bexhill, England

Weizmann House
1934–1937
Rehovot, Israel

Park Synagogue
1945–1953
Cleveland, Ohio

Erich Mendelsohn, *Poland–Germany*
1887–1953

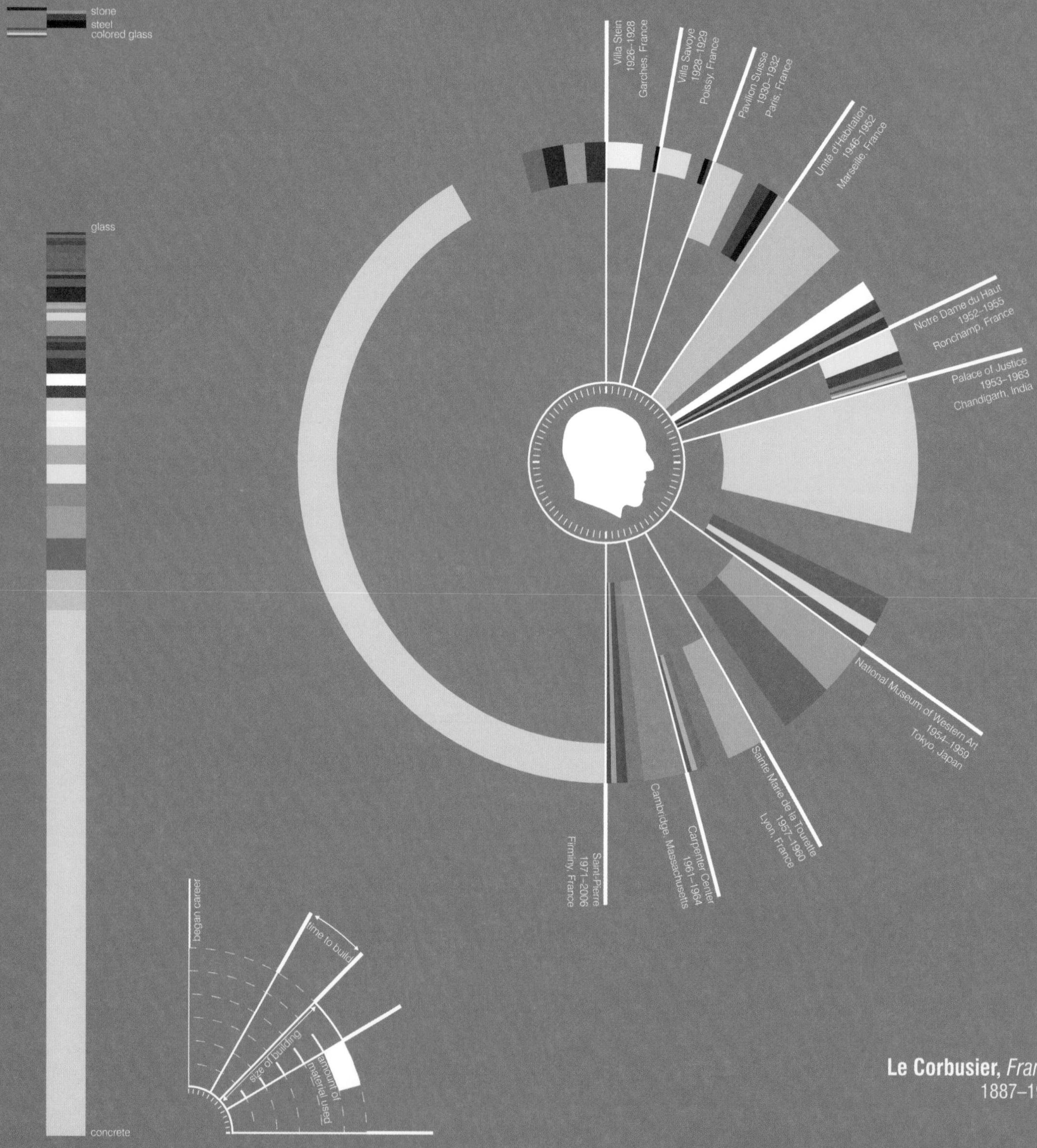

stone
steel
colored glass

glass

concrete

Villa Stein
1926–1928
Garches, France

Villa Savoye
1928–1929
Poissy, France

Pavillon Suisse
1930–1932
Paris, France

Unité d'Habitation
1946–1952
Marseille, France

Notre Dame du Haut
1952–1955
Ronchamp, France

Palace of Justice
1953–1963
Chandigarh, India

National Museum of Western Art
1954–1959
Tokyo, Japan

Sainte Marie de la Tourette
1957–1960
Lyon, France

Carpenter Center
1961–1964
Cambridge, Massachusetts

Saint-Pierre
1971–2006
Firminy, France

began career

time to build

size of building

amount of material used

Le Corbusier, *France*
1887–1965

150

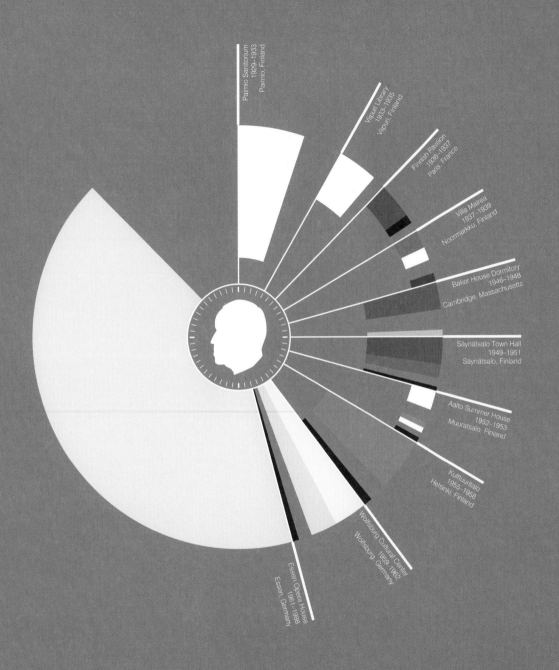

Alvar Aalto, *Finland*
1898–1976

tile
steel
marble
wood
brick
glass
concrete

Paimio Sanatorium
1929–1933
Paimio, Finland

Vipuri Library
1933–1935
Vipuri, Finland

Finnish Pavilion
1936–1937
Paris, France

Villa Mairea
1937–1939
Noormarkku, Finland

Baker House Dormitory
1946–1948
Cambridge, Massachusetts

Säynätsalo Town Hall
1949–1951
Säynätsalo, Finland

Aalto Summer House
1952–1953
Muuratsalo, Finland

Kulttuuritalo
1955–1958
Helsinki, Finland

Wolfsburg Cultural Center
1958–1962
Wolfsburg, Germany

Essen Opera House
1961–1988
Essen, Germany

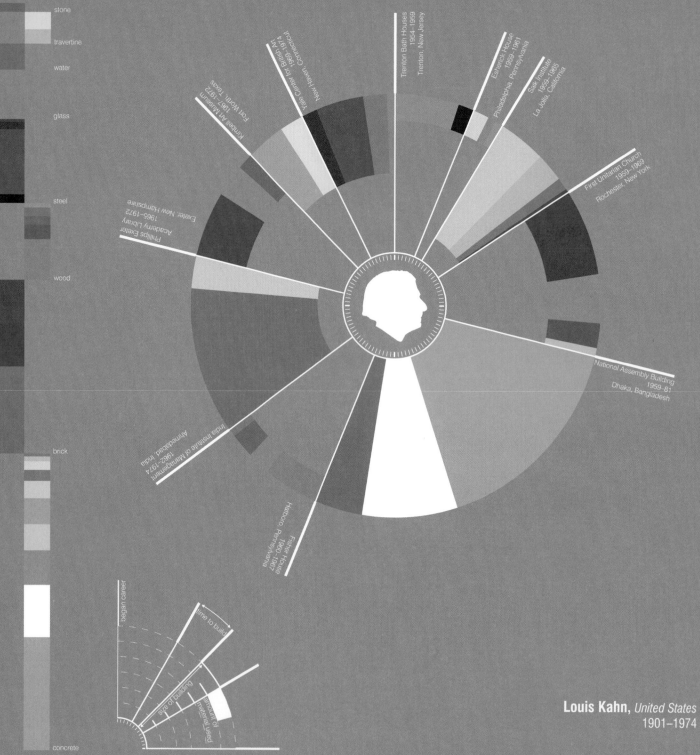

stone
travertine
water

glass

steel

wood

brick

concrete

Trenton Bath Houses
1954–1959
Trenton, New Jersey

Esherick House
1959–1961
Philadelphia, Pennsylvania

Salk Institute
1959–1965
La Jolla, California

First Unitarian Church
1959–1963
Rochester, New York

Yale Center for British Art
1969–1974
New Haven, Connecticut

Kimbell Art Museum
1967–1972
Fort Worth, Texas

Phillips Exeter
Academy Library
1965–1972
Exeter, New Hampshire

National Assembly Building
1959–81
Dhaka, Bangladesh

India Institute of Management
1962–1974
Ahmedabad, India

Fisher House
1960–1967
Hatboro, Pennsylvania

began career

time to build

size of building

amount of
material used

Louis Kahn, *United States*
1901–1974

152

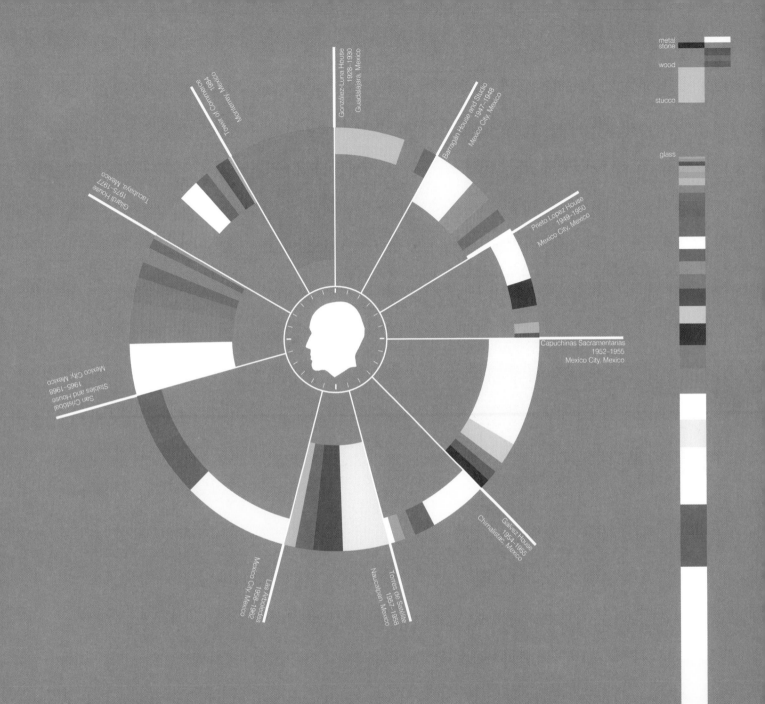

González-Luna House
1928–1930
Guadalajara, Mexico

Barragán House and Studio
1947–1948
Mexico City, Mexico

Prieto López House
1949–1950
Mexico City, Mexico

Tower of Commerce
1984
Monterrey, Mexico

Gilardi House
1975–1977
Tacubaya, Mexico

San Cristóbal
Stables and House
1965–1968
Mexico City, Mexico

Capuchinas Sacramentarias
1952–1955
Mexico City, Mexico

Las Arboledas
1958–1962
Mexico City, Mexico

Torres de Satélite
1957–1958
Naucalpan, Mexico

Gálvez House
1954–1955
Chimalistac, Mexico

metal
stone
wood
stucco

glass

concrete

Luis Barragán, *Mexico*
1902–1988

153

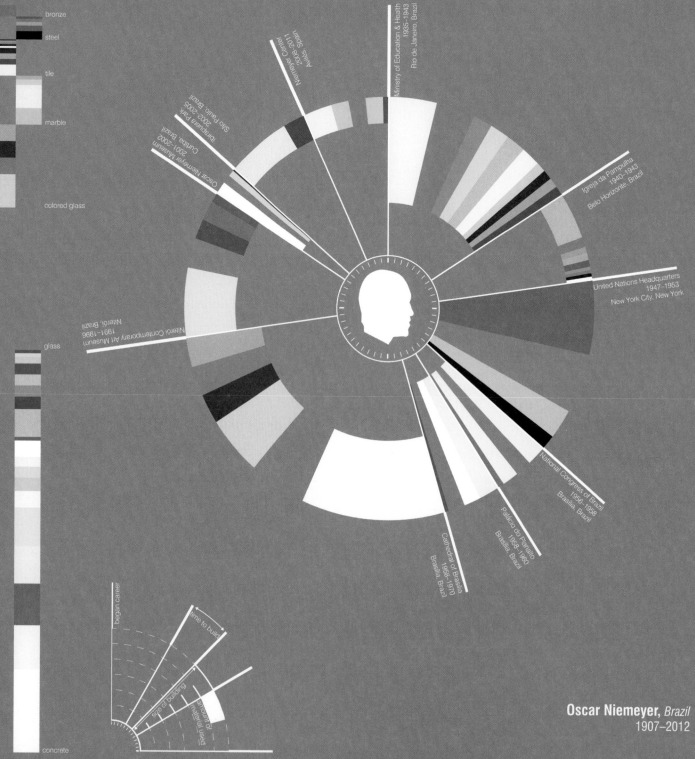

bronze
steel
tile
marble
colored glass

glass

concrete

Niemeyer Center 2008-2011
Avilés, Spain

Ministry of Education & Health
1936-1943
Rio de Janeiro, Brazil

Ibirapuera Park
2002-2005
São Paulo, Brazil

Oscar Niemeyer Museum
2001-2002
Curitiba, Brazil

Igreja da Pampulha
1940-1943
Belo Horizonte, Brazil

United Nations Headquarters
1947-1953
New York City, New York

Niterói Contemporary Art Museum
1991-1996
Niterói, Brazil

National Congress of Brazil
1956-1958
Brasília, Brazil

Palácio do Planalto
1958-1960
Brasília, Brazil

Cathedral of Brasília
1958-1970
Brasília, Brazil

began career
time to build
size of building
amount of material used

Oscar Niemeyer, *Brazil*
1907–2012

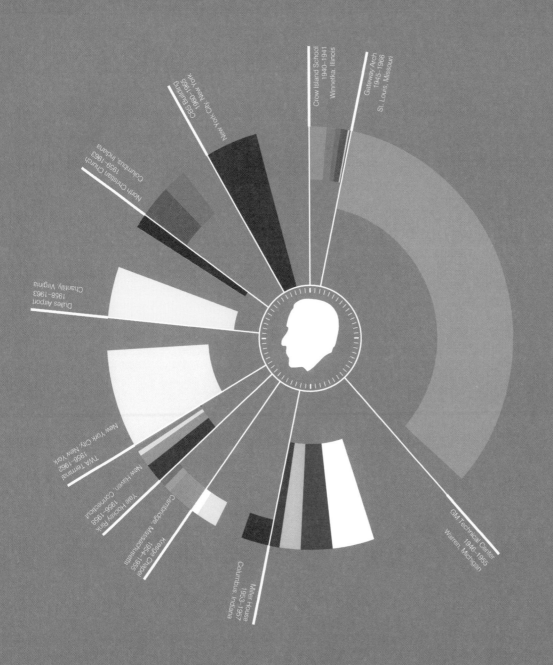

Crow Island School
1940–1941
Winnetka, Illinois

Gateway Arch
1945–1966
St. Louis, Missouri

CBS Building
1960–1965
New York City, New York

North Christian Church
1959–1963
Columbus, Indiana

Dulles Airport
1958–1963
Chantilly, Virginia

TWA Terminal
1956–1962
New York City, New York

Yale Hockey Rink
1956–1958
New Haven, Connecticut

Kresge Chapel
1954–1955
Cambridge, Massachusetts

Miller House
1953–1957
Columbus, Indiana

GM Technical Center
1946–1955
Warren, Michigan

water
brick
stone
metal
concrete
glass
stainless steel

Eero Saarinen, *Finland–United States*
1910–1961

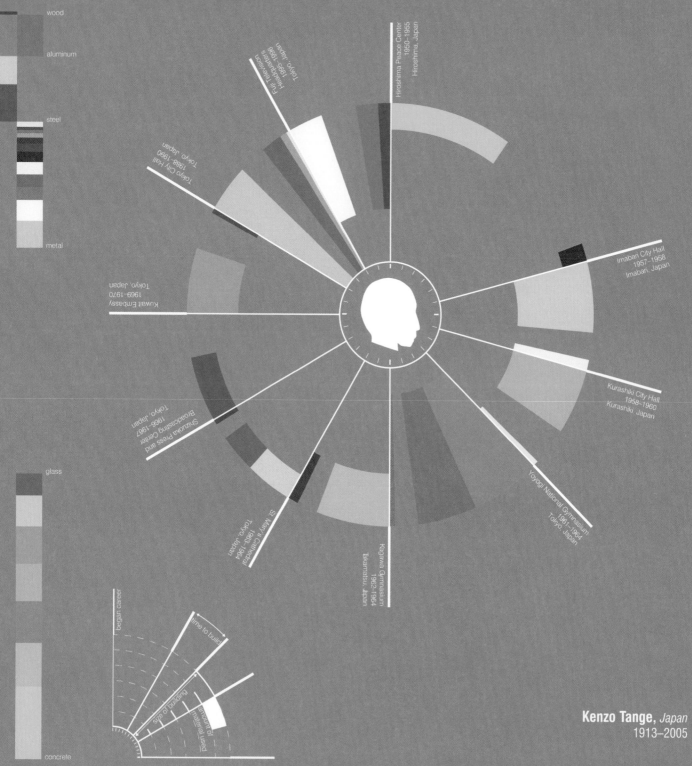

wood

aluminum

steel

metal

glass

concrete

Hiroshima Peace Center
1950–1955
Hiroshima, Japan

Fuji Television
Headquarters
1990–1996
Tokyo, Japan

Tokyo City Hall
1988–1990
Tokyo, Japan

Kuwait Embassy
1969–1970
Tokyo, Japan

Shizuoka Press and
Broadcasting Center
1966–1967
Tokyo, Japan

St. Mary's Cathedral
1963–1964
Tokyo, Japan

Kagawa Gymnasium
1962–1964
Takamatsu, Japan

Yoyogi National Gymnasium
1961–1964
Tokyo, Japan

Kurashiki City Hall
1958–1960
Kurashiki, Japan

Imaban City Hall
1957–1958
Imaban, Japan

began career

time to build

size of building

amount of
material used

Kenzo Tange, *Japan*
1913–2005

156

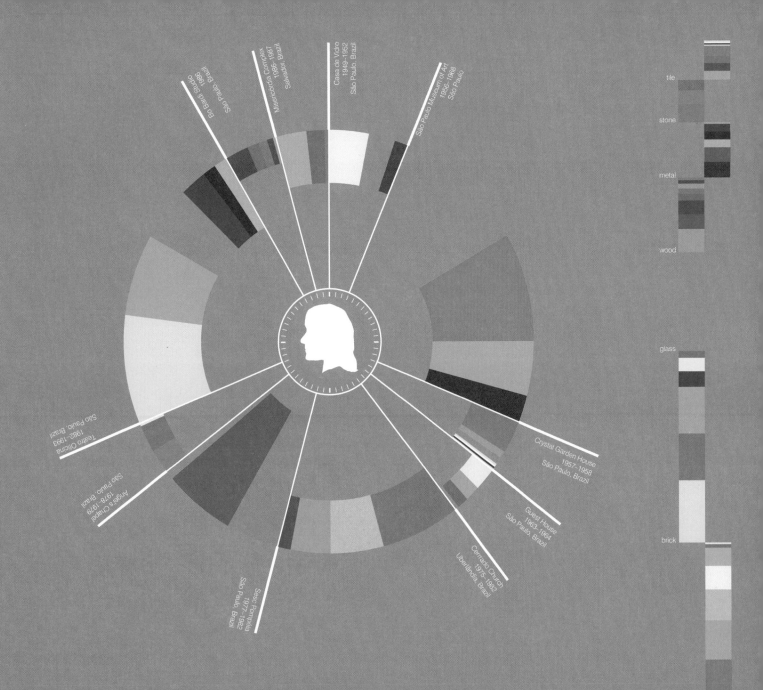

Bo Bardi Studio
1986, Brazil
São Paulo, Brazil

Misericórdia Complex
1986, 1987
Salvador, Brazil

Casa de Vidro
1949–1952
São Paulo, Brazil

São Paulo Museum of Art
1957–1968
São Paulo

Teatro Oficina
1982–1993
São Paulo, Brazil

Anjos's Chapel
1978–1979
São Paulo, Brazil

Sesc Pompéia
1977–1982
São Paulo, Brazil

Cerrado Church
1975–1982
Uberlândia, Brazil

Guest House
1963–1964
São Paulo, Brazil

Crystal Garden House
1957–1958
São Paulo, Brazil

tile

stone

metal

wood

glass

brick

concrete

Lina Bo Bardi, *Italy–Brazil*
1914–1992

157

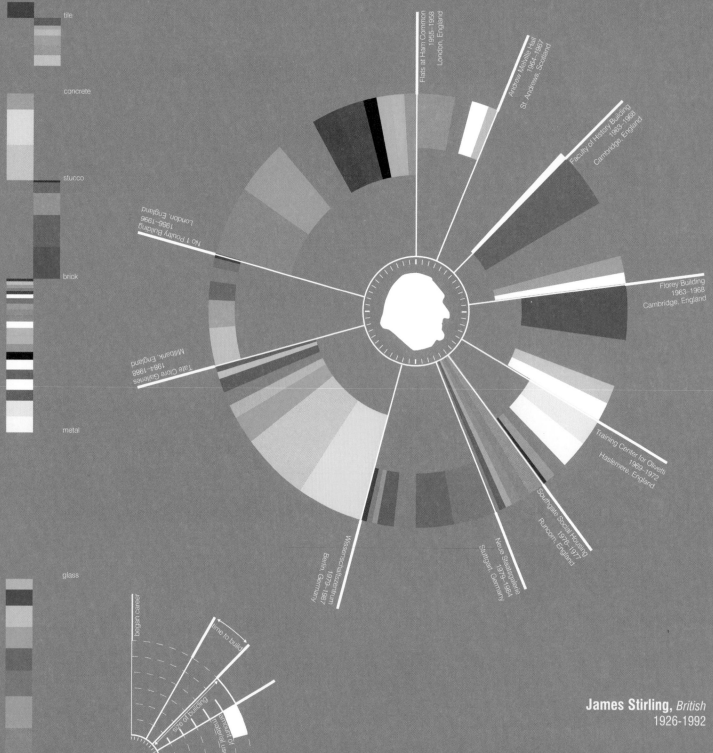

tile

concrete

stucco

brick

metal

glass

stone

Flats at Ham Common
1955-1958
London, England

Andrew Melville Hall
1964-1967
St. Andrews, Scotland

Faculty of History Building
1963-1968
Cambridge, England

Florey Building
1963-1968
Cambridge, England

Training Center for Olivetti
1969-1972
Haslemere, England

Southgate Social Housing
1976-1977
Runcorn, England

Neue Staatsgalerie
1979-1984
Stuttgart, Germany

Wissenschaftszentrum
1979-1987
Berlin, Germany

Tate Clore Galleries
1984-1988
Millbank, England

No. 1 Poultry Building
1986-1996
London, England

began career

time to build

size of building

amount of
material used

James Stirling, *British*
1926-1992

158

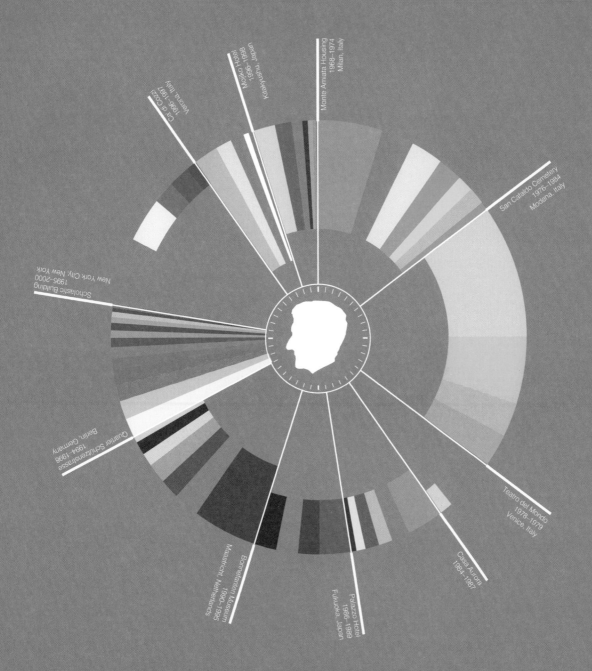

terra cotta

wood

brick

stone

glass

concrete

metal

stucco

Ca' di Cozzi
1986-1987
Verona, Italy

under construction
Molino Hotel
1996-1998
Klévarkush

Monte Amiata Housing
1968-1974
Milan, Italy

San Cataldo Cemetery
1976-1984
Modena, Italy

Scholastic Building
1995-2000
New York City, New York

Quartier Schützenstrasse
1994-1998
Berlin, Germany

Bonnefanten Museum
1990-1995
Maastricht, Netherlands

Palazzo Hotel
1986-1989
Fukuoka, Japan

Casa Aurora
1984-1987

Teatro del Mondo
1978-1979
Venice, Italy

Aldo Rossi, *Italian*
1931-1997

Acknowledgements

There are many people to thank who helped make *Archi-Graphic* a reality. First, a tremendous amount of thanks is owed to the students at The University of Arkansas Fay Jones School of Architecture, who became part of the early team that attacked the first diagrams of the book with a feverish energy. It was likely the combination of pizza, soda and late-night critiques after studio that made the early work so rich. Specifically, I'd like to thank (in alphabetical order) Thomas Boyster, Morgan Conway, Patricia Della Serra, Eric Dethamphaivan, Kate Edwards, Jonathan Evans, Molly Evans, Ethan Fowler, Edmundo Gonzalez, Caitlyn Juarez, Colby Leding, Christian Linares, Juan Martinez, Quinten McElvain, Kelley Reed, Colby Ritter, Iyppi Ryan, Andrew Schalk, and Virginia Singh Del Rio, who spent many hours deciphering sketches, digitizing drawings, and exhaustively discussing ideas throughout the creation process. Special thanks are owed to two of the students listed above, Kelley Reed and Ethan Fowler, who were instrumental forces without which the book would likely be a shadow of its current self. Many thanks are also owed to The University of Arkansas and the Fay Jones School of Architecture who were both very supportive of the project. Finally, thank you to my wife Emilie and my sons Topher and Benny for putting up with my absence from home while working on the project; I hope that opening and meandering through the book's pages will help you recapture some of that lost energy.